Researching the Legal Web

The Authors

Nick Holmes is an electronic publishing consultant specialising in the legal sector. He has more than 20 years' experience in legal publishing and, since the early days of the PC, has been involved in the electronic processing and publication of legal reference texts.

Nick set up as an independent consultant in the late 80s, advising publishers on and implementing text management and electronic publishing solutions. In 1991 he formed Information for Lawyers Ltd (IFL) who provide electronic publishing services to law publishers and products and services directly to over 1,800 lawyers.

Nick has monitored the development of the 'UK legal web' from its birth, and developed and maintains the first UK legal web gateway on the *infolaw* website at www.infolaw.co.uk. He also writes a monthly 'Page on the Web' column for the *Solicitors' Journal* and occasional articles in other lawtech journals.

Contact NickHolmes@infolaw.co.uk or telephone 020 8878 3033.

Delia Venables is a computer consultant specialising in legal systems. Since becoming an independent consultant over 10 years ago, she has advised well over 100 firms of solicitors on their computer and word processing requirements, many of them more than once, as they have upgraded or replaced their systems.

For several years Delia Venables was the Law Society's consultant in setting up and operating the Recognition Procedure for Computer Systems for Solicitors. She continues to write for Law Society publications and she is a Law Society listed consultant. She is a Fellow of the British Computer Society and served for several years on the Expert Systems Specialist Group.

She has developed a special expertise in the internet and has written and published *A Guide to the Internet for Lawyers* which includes the Internet Tutorials for Lawyers. She also publishes the *Internet Newsletter* which keeps lawyers up to date in this fast moving field. She writes regularly for the journal of the Society for Computers and Law.

Her website at www.venables.co.uk/legal/ is widely acknowledged as one of the principal legal portal sites on the web, linking to all the important legal resources which are available, as they appear.

Contact delia@venables.co.uk or telephone 01273 472424.

Researching the Legal Web

A guide to legal resources on the internet

Second Edition

Nick Holmes

Delia Venables

Butterworths
London, Dublin, Edinburgh
1999

UNITED KINGDOM Butterworths a Division of Reed Elsevier (UK) Ltd,
Halsbury House, 35 Chancery Lane,
London WC2A 1EL and
4 Hill Street, Edinburgh EH2 3JZ
AUSTRALIA Butterworths, Sydney, Melbourne, Brisbane,
Adelaide, Perth, Canberra and Hobart
CANADA Butterworths Canada Ltd, Toronto and Vancouver
IRELAND Butterworths Ireland Ltd, Dublin
MALAYSIA Malayan Law Journal Sdn Bhd, Kuala Lumpur
NEW ZEALAND Butterworths of New Zealand Ltd, Wellington
and Auckland
SINGAPORE Reed Elsevier (Singapore) Pte Ltd, Singapore
SOUTH AFRICA Butterworth Publishers (Pty) Ltd, Durban
USA Michie, Charlottesville, Virginia

Typeset by Information for Lawyers Ltd, London
Printed by Redwood Books, Trowbridge, Wiltshire

Contents

Preface

When we wrote the first edition of this book, over the summer of 1997, there was already an enormous amount of information available on the web for lawyers. The last two years have seen this multiply many times, both in variety and quantity, and what was then a useful but limited information resource is now at the very centre of modern legal research and practice.

The law publishers, in 1997, were concerned that they should be present on the web with at least some part of their published resources. Now, they are only too aware that any publisher who does not provide the vast majority of its available material on the web will very soon be dead. Indeed, the question in the board rooms must surely have shifted from 'Should we put material onto the web?' to 'Should we still publish material in hard copy form?' Similarly, librarians in legal firms will no longer be asking 'Do we need to provide web access to these materials as well as buying the books?' but 'Which resources are better provided online (and possibly on the firm's intranet) rather than in book or journal form?'

In Government departments the question 'How can we justify the resources needed to provide a web presence?' will have changed to 'How can we satisfy the Prime Minister's instruction that 25% of the government's interaction with the citizen should be carried out on the web by 2002?'

Amongst firms of solicitors, the argument has shifted from 'Should we take any notice of this thing called the web?' to 'If we do not work out how to provide at least some of our legal services on the web, we will lose a serious amount of our business.' Furthermore, many legal advisors, at least those who deal in cutting edge cases, cannot now afford to say 'I know my way round the printed resources better than the online ones' as they must ask themselves 'Will we be found negligent if we do not know what happened in the courts yesterday?'

Against this background we have attempted to bring together the most important legal resources, both research and practice-based, as well as many examples illustrating how lawyers are using the web to develop their practice. We hope that this book will assist lawyers both in the daily grind and in planning for the future.

We are indebted to our guest authors who have covered several topics in a way which we ourselves could not have done. These include a description of, respectively, Scottish and Irish legal resources on the web, a detailed review of legal research services on the web, a description of how the Lord Chancellor's Department website is developing, legal education on the web and several case studies of how firms and chambers are marketing themselves, or providing legal services, on the web.

Nick Holmes and Delia Venables
30 September 1999

Chapter 1

Introduction

Contents

This chapter describes how to use this book to access the 'UK legal web', particularly in conjunction with our own websites which complement it. Some concepts and jargon which you will encounter in this book and on the web are also explained.

We use the term 'UK legal web' to refer to those UK lawyers and law related organisations who have sites on the web and those sites which are designed for or will be of immediate use to UK lawyers. Having said that, in this edition we do also cover the Republic of Ireland.

Further reading

This book assumes that the reader has a basic understanding of the internet. For less experienced users, we suggest the *Guide to the Internet for Lawyers*, by Delia Venables. This helps the lawyer get started and includes a set of Internet Tutorials for Lawyers which qualifies for CPD hours from the Law Society of England and Wales, the Law Society of Scotland, the Bar Council (New Practitioner Programme) and the Institute of Legal Executives. This costs £60 or £75.70 to include a year's subscription to the *Internet Newsletter for Lawyers*.

The *Internet Newsletter for Lawyers* covers ongoing topics similar to the ones in this book and costs £34.70 for a year's subscription (6 issues) or £60 plus VAT for loading onto an intranet. Contact Delia Venables on 01273 472424 or delia@venables.co.uk.

For the **Law of the Internet** we suggest the following:

Internet Law and Regulation, edited by Graham Smith of Bird & Bird, Sweet & Maxwell 1997, £85 (second edition). This detailed and informative book covers Intellectual Property, Defamation, Content Liability and Protection, Data Protection, Telecommunications and Broadcast Regulation, Contracts, Payment Mechanisms, Prohibited and Regulated Activities, and Taxation.

The Laws of the Internet, by Clive Gringras, then at Nabarro Nathanson, Butterworths 1997, ISBN 0 406 00249 5, £85. The book covers Contract, Tort, Intellectual Property, Crime, Data Protection, Taxation, Securities and Financial Services, Competition and Banking.

E-Commerce: Law & Practice, by Michael Chissick and Alistair Kelman, Sweet & Maxwell 1999, £125, ISBN 0752 006509. This focuses on the UK and European regulatory and compliance issues to be considered when doing business online in Europe.

Digital Media – Contracts, Rights and Licensing, by lawyers at Denton Hall, Sweet & Maxwell 1998, £120, ISBN 075200 4204. The first edition of this book was called 'Multimedia', but the topic has developed to cover all types of digital products.

Structure and Content of the Book

- This chapter describes how this book can be used to access the 'UK legal web' and how it is complemented by our own websites.

- Chapter 2 looks at the lawyers and law-related organisations who are on the web, including solicitors, barristers, groups and associations, Government departments and agencies, Parliament and the Courts.

- Chapter 3 describes the types of resources available for lawyers: from legislation and cases through to jobs online.

- Chapter 4 reviews the services provided by law publishers – from the large and long-established to the smaller and newer.

- Chapter 5 serves as an index to the most useful UK websites specialising in particular areas of law and practice, classified by topic.

- Chapter 6 gives guidance on using internet search engines and 'portals' to find information on the web.

- Chapters 7 and 8 look at e-commerce for lawyers – on the one hand, buying goods and services, and on the other, marketing and selling legal services on the web.

- Chapter 9 provides an introduction to intranets (internal webs) and extranets.

- Chapter 10 covers legal education on the web, including law schools, online tuition, student resources, careers and CPD.

- Chapters 11 and 12 describe resources available specifically for Scotland and the Republic of Ireland.

- Chapter 13 is concerned with international legal resources, including 'global' resources and sites concerned with the principal overseas jurisdictions of interest to the UK lawyer.

We are only too aware that no two individuals can adequately cover all the material of interest to lawyers on the web. We therefore invited a number of guest authors to contribute articles to complement our efforts and these are presented, with accreditation, as sections within the appropriate chapters.

The book is liberally illustrated with screenshots of the sites under discussion: the web is very much a visual medium and often a view of even a part of website will speak louder than our descriptions. Of course, the monochrome illustrations do not do justice to some of the more adventurous sites.

Concepts and Jargon

We have tried to keep the commentary simple and non-technical, but no book on this topic can avoid using terms which, since they have not been long in the public domain, are unfamiliar to some. Following, therefore, is a brief explanation of the many recurring terms used (shown in *italics*), in the context of a condensed summary of what the web is, how it works and how it is used. More experienced users may skip this section.

The *web* (or WWW, short for World Wide Web) is a seamlessly linked mass of information stored on millions of computers around the world which are connected to the *internet* (a network of computer networks). Computers which supply information over the internet are known as *servers*. Information is stored as *pages* written in a language called *html* (hypertext markup language) which is understood and interpreted by the viewing software on your computer called a web *browser* – *Netscape* and Microsoft Internet *Explorer* are the leading examples. Pages essentially contain text, but may also incorporate graphics or sound or even video clips.

Most importantly pages also contain *links* – computer code which activates a jump to another section of that page or a *request* to the server for another page which may be stored on the same server or on any other server on the internet. Links are usually displayed as coloured and/or underlined text, but may also be wrapped around images, or be activated by a button or a defined area of an *image map*. Links can also activate programs which will perform useful tasks, such as searching a database or sending a message. Increasingly web publishers are also using computer programs written in new languages such as *Java* or *ActiveX* which, rather than performing their wizardry on the *host* computer, are downloaded in small fragments and activated on *your* computer. These techniques are fascinating to web developers, but often irritating to the user, producing a busy screen and sometimes causing your system to crash.

Each page on the web has a unique *address*, also referred to as a *URL* (uniform resource locator). For more on URLs, see p 6.

Web pages will often be divided into *frames* – independently scrollable areas of the screen. Usually, one narrow frame will contain a menu whose links will load pages into the main frame; all sorts of things may be happening in other frames. Used with restraint frames can be an aid to navigation of a site, but overused they defeat this object. They also reduce the amount of screen space available for the main page.

On the subject of *screens* (or *displays*), size doesn't matter *per se*: what matter more when viewing the web are your screen settings. If you are wondering why many web pages fall off the right hand side of your screen or have bad breaks in headings, you are probably using a display setting of 640 × 480 pixels: most web pages are now designed to be displayed with an 800 × 600 setting. You can easily change settings: in Windows 95 select Control Panel, Settings, Display.

Many websites provide materials which you can *download*, ie transfer from the host system and save on your local machine. These may be text or word processor files which you can load in your word processor, programs which you can download and install, or any other file. Usually, if they are large files, they will be in a compressed file format. *Zip* files are the most popular format (ie files have the extension .zip); you require a copy of PKZip or WinZip installed in order to decompress them. But often Zip files are supplied as self-extracting .exe files, in which case all you need do is run the file.

pdf format is also common, particularly where the information has already been produced as a printed document – this is Adobe's Portable Document Format. To view pdf files you need the Adobe Acrobat reader installed, available from Adobe's website at www.adobe.com – often a copy or a link to Adobe's site will be provided on the site which offers the pdf files. Pdf is most commonly employed as a way of publishing forms and leaflets – see further p 59.

Accessing the Websites

In this book the names of websites are printed in **bold** type. At the head of each section is given the URL on one or both of the authors' sites where links to the sites mentioned will be found. In guest articles and other sections where links may not readily be found on our web pages, URLs for each site are quoted.

URLs are quoted without the http:// prefix to avoid irritation. The prefix is in any event unnecessary as current browsers will assume it by default.

Wherever possible, for the purposes of this book and our web pages, we have gathered the URLs from the page loaded in our browsers and pasted them into the text – to avoid the risk of error and outdated references. However, errors there nevertheless may be, and if for this or other reason you cannot load a page cited, or wish to access a page at a higher level, an understanding of the makeup of a URL is essential.

The first part of the URL after the http:// is the server name, comprising usually 'www' plus the domain name, eg www.bigco.co.uk. If you wish to access the home page of Big Co you can usually use just this part. However, you may need to type a user directory name as well: for example to access Delia Venables' home page you need to access www.venables.co.uk/legal/. (Note that, as here, punctuation often follows quoted URLs and is not part of the address.)

The remainder of a web address is the path and filename of the page, with directories (folders) separated by forward slashes (rather than backslashes as is the Windows convention). Filenames have the extension .htm or .html. Most directories will have a default page that will be loaded if you do not explicitly quote a page name; thus usually pages named index.html, default.html or welcome.html need not be typed.

Knowing these rules it is straightforward to access pages at a higher level if you encounter an error in accessing a specific page or simply want to investigate further up the tree: delete the last part of the address up to the slash and try that address. If there is no default page you may get a directory listing, or an 'access prohibited' message. Proceed accordingly, either to select the page required or to try again at the next level up. Happy surfing!

The Authors' Websites

To access the sites mentioned in this book you need only two essential book-marks – those of our sites. We have each, independently, maintained websites for over four and a half years with broadly the same intent: to provide lawyers and their clients with a jumping-off point for their research, as well, of course, as advertising our respective services.

Our researches over this period, reflected in the classified sets of links and other services we have constructed, have formed the basis for this book.

To access the sites described in this book therefore, simply access one or other of our home pages and follow the obvious links to the relevant part of the site.

Nick Holmes

www.infolaw.co.uk

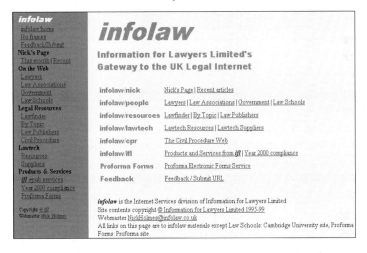

The infolaw site which I maintain for my company Information for Lawyers Ltd started off in late 1994 as a set of personal bookmarks. A few months later I had learned enough to publish it as a set of web pages whose primary aim remains to attract visits from lawyers and those who service them by providing a valuable free resource. Through the site we have established and developed relationships with lawyers, suppliers and service providers which have contributed substantially to the overall development of the business. Little money actually changes hands on the site, but the value of the site to the company and to me personally cannot be overestimated.

The site largely comprises classified indexes of links to lawyers and legal and law-tech resources. It is of straightforward design and avoids the use of graphics and large pages. This ensures speedy navigation and quick loading. The primary pages are all accessible from the side menu frame. Although this frame remains when accessing external sites, it may be overridden by selecting the No Frames option (or by bookmarking the unframed page www.infolaw.co.uk/home.htm) – in which case I leave it to you to use your Back button.

The pages are currently grouped under the following headings:

- **infolaw/people** provides access to websites of lawyers and law-related organisations on the web: Government on the Web, Lawyers on the Web and Associations on the Web. The Lawyers pages include links to all UK and Irish lawyers' sites, including separate indexes for law firms in England & Wales, Scotland, Northern Ireland, Republic of Ireland, law firm groups, and barristers. All bona fide UK and Irish law firms and chambers with websites are invited to submit their details for inclusion on the feedback form provided.

- **infolaw/resources** provides three indexes for accessing resources on the web of specific use to UK lawyers. Lawfinder provides convenient tabular access to sites hosting free primary law, with direct links also to their update and search pages; the Legal Resources by Topics page indexes the most useful sites in specific areas of law and practice; and the Law Publishers page provides links to the principal law publishers' web services (though on the web we are all publishers now).

- **infolaw/lawtech** provides links to a wide range of useful legal technology sites and a separate listing of suppliers of legal technology products in the UK.

- **infolaw/cpr** The Civil Procedure Web provides links to primary materials relating to the Civil Procedure Rules and a host of useful commentary sites, together with an online update. Information for Lawyers' own CPR product, distributed on CD is also online for subscribers.

- **infolaw/nick** includes Nick's page on the Web – comment and analysis of developments in the UK legal web which I write monthly for the *Solicitors Journal* – and other articles occasionally contributed to other journals such as *Computers & Law* and Delia Venables' *Internet Newsletter for Lawyers*.

- **Proforma Forms** is a separate website of Information for Lawyers' sister company Proforma Ltd. On this site is news, information and links regarding official law forms, with 20 free downloadable forms in HotDocs format (see further p 59).

Delia Venables

www.venables.co.uk/legal/

	Portal to Legal Resources in the UK and Ireland, maintained by Delia Venables		
Free Legal Information for Individuals	Free Legal Information for Companies	Information for Solicitors and Barristers	September/October issue of the Internet Newsletter for Lawyers!

Legal Sites and Resources in the UK *Last updated on September 10th.* *(Scottish resources last updated 3rd September).*	New! The most significant new sites. *Last updated on September 14th.*
Legal Sites and Resources in Ireland *Last updated on August 20th.*	Free Legal Current Awareness Sources *Last updated on September 10th.*
On-line Services from the Legal Publishers *Last updated on August 25th.*	Selling Legal Services Online! *Last updated on September 10th.*
Solicitors in England: A to E, F to J, K to Q, R to Z *Last updated on September 2nd.* Scotland, Wales, Northern Ireland, Off-shore and Ireland Also, Law Firm Groups	Barristers in the UK: A-G.....H-Z *Last updated on September 10th.* Barristers in Ireland
Legal Sites and Resources in Other Countries Europe, USA, Canada, Australia, New Zealand, China, Japan	Around the World Wide Web in 80 minutes A tour of some interesting legal sites

My main business is advising solicitors and barristers on their computer requirements, including networking, accounts and time recording, integrated systems, case management, client data base, marketing and voice recognition. I spend my time visiting firms around the country, mainly high street firms, and helping them decide on their IT strategy.

In early 1995 I 'discovered' the Internet and was immediately captivated by the opportunities it offered and the use which the legal profession could make of it. My web pages started to offer a series of short cuts to legal resources as they appeared and the internet became a second and (progressively) an equal part of my working life.

When Nick and I wrote the first edition of this book, two years ago, these two strands were largely separate; very few high street firms had developed much interest in the Internet and it was the larger firms, not generally my clients, who became the readers of my publications and the ones using the website.

Now, the two strands are coming together and firms of all sizes are not only looking at the web to find legal resources set up by others, but are actively investigating what use they can make of the web for marketing their services and for selling their services online.

My website covers a large array of legal resources, including:

- **Free Legal Information for Individuals** – links to resources made available, mainly by solicitors, on topics like accidents and injuries, benefits, consumer issues, conveyancing, crime police and prisons, and many other topics.

- **Free Legal Information for Companies** – a compendium of the resources made available by solicitors on business and commercial topics.
- **Legal Sites and Resources in the UK**, categorised in major subject areas like business and commercial topics, charities, civil justice, computer and internet law, construction, and so on.
- **Legal Sites and Resources in Ireland**.
- **Online Services from the Legal Publishers** – descriptions of what services are offered for legal research online.
- **Free Legal Current Awareness Sources**, covering not only what the publishers have to offer, but also legal sources in newspapers and free case reports from firms and chambers.
- **Solicitors**, and also **Barristers**, with their own websites – many hundreds of these now. There is also a special section indicating which firms are selling legal services online.
- **Legal IT Suppliers**, with descriptions of what each supplier has to offer, and **Web Services Companies** offering services to the legal profession.
- **Student Resources**, Legal Training and Courses, including CPD courses.
- Also, Groups and Associations of Individual Lawyers, Expert Witnesses, Arbitration Resources, Jobs and Recruitment Opportunities, News and Newspapers, International Resources and Year 2000 resources.
- Information on my own publications – the *Internet Newsletter for Lawyers* and the *Guide to the Internet for Lawyers* (see p 2 for more on these).

Chapter 2

Who's on the Legal Web?

Contents

Government

Links to Government sites are at www.infolaw.co.uk/ifl/govt.htm

Almost all Government departments and agencies are now on the web. These sites have moved at varying pace from brochure ('this is who we are'), to information source ('here is what we publish'), to – in some cases – transactional services. All these sites can be found via the indispensable CCTA Government Information Service site (see below). This section describes briefly the principal law-related Government sites on the web. Other Government sites are mentioned under the appropriate topic headings in Chapter 5. As to law and other information resources published by Government, see Chapter 3.

The Government Information Service

The **Central Computer and Telecommunications Agency** (CCTA) **Government Information Service** is the starting point for Government departments and agencies and hundreds of related organisations. These can be accessed by Organisation Name and by Function. There is also a mechanism to search across the CCTA databases which include all UK Government servers, including local government.

The What's New section includes information on many new Government press releases, reports and initiatives. The Organisation and Function indexes do not claim to be comprehensive and should thus be regarded as good starting points rather than definitive lists. However, this is a very impressive site and one which is continuing to develop fast.

Government departments and agencies

The **Cabinet Office** site 'aims to provide you with the fastest and fullest access to information published by the Cabinet Office'. There is extensive information on all aspects of the work of the Cabinet, including Ministers and organisation, support committees, public sector standards, guidance and consultation papers, the Government machine, the Civil Service and issues which span the boundaries of Government. The main omission is a summary of the role of the Cabinet Office!

The **Central Office of Information** (COI) site hosts the texts of all Government press releases, offering a What's New Today page, a Search by Date facility and an alphabetical list of links to the press releases organised by organisation (more than 65 of them). There are in fact two press release websites: the new press release site provides a searchable database of releases going back to the beginning of 1998, and is updated in three batches each working day; the old site provides a comprehensive archive of press releases from April 1995 to the present day.

The **Charity Commission** 'is here to give the public confidence in the integrity of charities'. It provides the texts of most of its leaflets and press releases on its pages plus the Register of Charities, searchable by name, object geographical area or number.

The **Court Service** website is described on p 26.

The **Crown Prosecution Service** (CPS) is the Government Department which prosecutes people in England and Wales who have been charged by the police with a criminal offence. It:

- provides a national framework and standards
- provides support for the work of the Branches with advice
- plays an important part in shaping the Government's criminal justice policy
- maintains contact with key Government departments

The site contains information on the role and activities of the CPS and a News Desk. Publications on the site include the Code for Crown Prosecutors.

The **Data Protection Registrar**'s pages include Guidance Notes, information on Registration, a Data Protection Summary and other information.

Publications on the site include Data Protection Guidelines and an Introduction to the Data Protection Act 1998, and there is a host of links to data protection and telecommunications directives, regulations and papers.

Also on the site is the complete Data Protection Register with the facility to search it on Name or Registration Number.

The **HM Customs & Excise** site is divided into two sections: for the public (eg you returning from holiday) and for businesses (you at your desk). The latter has a substantial amount of information on VAT, Customs, Excise and Intrastat, including most Customs & Excise leaflets and other publications. These and many of their forms are presented in Adobe pdf format.

HM Land Registry is the government department responsible for keeping and maintaining the Land Register of England and Wales. Its main purpose is to register title to land in England and Wales and to record dealings once the land is registered.

The site carries information on Property Price Reports, the Direct Access Service, Areas Served, Regional Offices, Lodging Applications and Fees. The Land Registry produces a wide range of publications from Explanatory Leaflets to the Residential Property Price Report. Documents on the site are available in either pdf format, as web pages or both.

The Areas Served is a list of links for all the District and Unitary Authorities in England and Wales. Clicking on a link brings up the name and address details of the District Land Registry which serves that authority – a useful bookmark for any conveyancer.

The **Registers of Scotland** (ROS) pages describe the history and workings of the Scottish registers. The site also includes a news page and sets out a table of the registration fees.

Though the trading businesses of the former **HMSO** were sold to the National Publishing Group in 1996 and now trade as The Stationery Office Ltd, the Controller of HMSO undertook certain functions on behalf of the Crown which were not undertaken by Parliament or any nominated Government department, and

HMSO has therefore been retained as a residuary body with the following principal functions:

- Responsibility for Acts of Parliament, Church of England Measures and Statutory Instruments and Measures of the Northern Ireland Assembly.

- Superintendence of the London, Edinburgh and Belfast Gazettes.

- Editorial responsibilities for some Statutory Publications previously undertaken within the Statutory Publications Office.

- Co-ordination of the publication of Command Papers and other publications within the House of Commons Numbered Series.

- Control and administration of Crown copyright and administration of Parliamentary copyright.

HMSO's website is host to all recent Acts and SIs (see p 52) and the putative Information Asset Register (see p 64). There is also important information and guidance notes on Crown copyright.

HM Treasury formulates and puts into effect the UK Government's financial and economic policy. Information on its website includes daily news releases, budget information, economic forecasts, consultation documents, the panel of Independent Forecaster's reports, a tax ready reckoner and ministers' speeches.

The Budget information page covers all recent budgets, and, at the appropriate time of year, the current Finance Bill, explanatory notes and downloadable bundles of Budget documents.

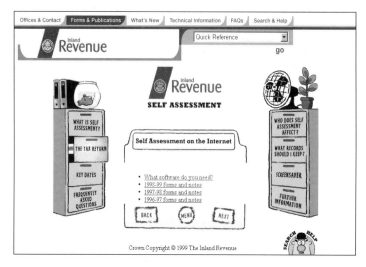

Crown Copyright © 1999 The Inland Revenue

The **Inland Revenue** is responsible, under the overall direction of Treasury Ministers, for the efficient administration of income tax, national insurance contributions, corporation tax, capital gains tax, petroleum revenue tax, inheritance tax and stamp duties. The Department's aim is to provide an effective and fair service to the country and Government. Its site is an extensive set of pages. The Tax for Businesses section includes the following:

- Self Assessment – comprehensive information on all aspects of self assessment.
- Construction Industry Scheme – changes to taxation within the construction industry affecting both contractors and sub-contractors.
- Corporation Tax Self Assessment – which companies are affected, recent developments.
- Year 2000 – information on preparedness and date-handling policy.
- Employer's Pack – guidance and tables to assist employers/payroll agents in completing employer annual returns and operating PAYE/NICs schemes.
- Forms and Publications – self assessment forms in Adobe pdf format, plus a range of leaflets and booklets explaining different areas of tax in plain English.
- Technical Information – documents on tax law and reviews of taxation practices; draft regulations, feedback documents, statutory instruments, tax bulletins, the Code of Practice on Consultation, customer service standards, and magnetic media and electronic data interchange.

On the **Law Commission** site you can find out more about the Commission; see details of the law currently being reviewed by the Commission in the areas of Common Law, Company & Commercial Law, Criminal Law, Property & Trust

Law, Statute Law; and browse or download the summaries and full text of the Commission's recent publications.

The **Legal Aid Board** has an extensive site with separate sections for the members of the public seeking legal aid, and lawyers.

Under the Seeking Legal Aid section there are html versions of all the Board's leaflets concerning eligibility, the statutory charge, customer service and franchising. These are convenient for the viewer to read and print from the computer, as needed.

The section for lawyers provides detailed information on the Regional Legal Services Committees, Franchising (including the current Legal Aid Franchise Quality Assurance Standard), Contracting, Guidance on the Exercise of Devolved Powers, Plans for Development, including the Legal Services Commission (LSC), the Community Legal Service (CLS) and the Criminal Defence Service (CDS), the LAB offices, consultation papers, forms and leaflets. Where the documents are substantial ones, they are provided in pdf format.

The site is well designed and informative and avoids programming gimmicks and fussy elements. The board promises to keep the site up to date with news and information on new developments and consultations.

The **Scottish Legal Aid Board** site answers similar questions for those north of the border. The main frame area is irritatingly small.

The **Lord Chancellor's Department** is responsible for the effective management of the courts; the appointment of judges, magistrates and other judicial office holders; the administration of legal aid; and the oversight of a varied programme of Government civil legislation and reform in such as family law, property law, defamation and legal aid. The site provides access to a wide range of materials on these subjects and the complete text of the Civil Procedure Rules (see further p 57).

See also the article by Mike Wicksteed on the development of the LCD site on p 21.

The main roles of the **Office of Fair Trading** (OFT) are to identify and put right trading practices which are against the consumer's interests; regulate the provision of consumer credit; and act directly on the activities of industry and commerce by investigating and remedying anti-competitive practices and abuses of market power and bringing about market structures which encourage competitive behaviour.

On its website you will find information on the work of the OFT; copies of its reports and press releases; news stories and articles from Fair Trading magazine; reference material on its past and present interests in consumer protection and competition policy, and advice on the rights of UK consumers.

The **Official Solicitor** describes its role as 'represent[ing] persons under legal disability, or deceased, or unascertained, as a party to a civil court action, when no other suitable person is able and willing to act, for the purpose of preventing a possible denial of justice and/or safeguarding the welfare, property or status of the person under disability.' There is a comprehensive set of information and leaflets available from the site.

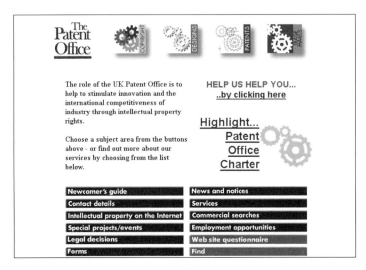

The **Patent Office** site provides much useful information on Patents, Trade Marks, Designs and Copyright and a section on Intellectual Property on the Internet and also includes many useful links to other intellectual property organisations. Of particular note are the publication of:

- All decisions issued by the Patent Office since the beginning of 1998, with selected historical decisions added as and when resources permit.
- A wide range of Patent, Supplementary Protection, Trade Mark, Design and Design Right forms and Fee Sheets.

The decisions and forms are all published in Adobe pdf format.

The **Social Security and Child Support Commissioners** are the specialised part of the Judiciary appointed to determine appeals.

On their pages you can find:

- A description of the work of the Commissioners.
- A list of the present Commissioners.
- Recent Commissioners' decisions.

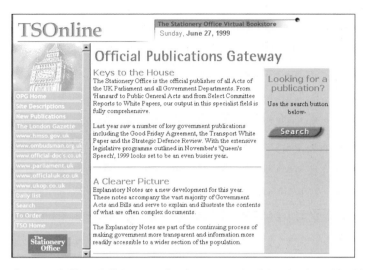

The **Stationery Office** (TSO) completely reorganised its site in mid-1999.

Built upon firm foundations following the privatisation of HMSO in October 1996 and the subsequent major investment in the latest technology and skills, The Stationery Office is a major publishing resource. We have a long history of publishing statutory, parliamentary and governmental information and have been the UK's official publisher to Parliament for more than 200 years. We are also the UK's largest publisher by volume, developing some 11,000 books, CDs and websites every year including The Highway Code, British Pharmacopoeia and Whitaker's Almanack TM. In addition, The Stationery Office is the publisher of the UK's only official newspapers- The London Gazette (the world's oldest daily newspaper) and the Belfast and Edinburgh Gazettes.

Amongst a wealth of confusing menus are the following useful elements to the site:

- An Official Publications Gateway, providing links to all official publications sites.

- A Search facility eanbling you to search for any TSO publication either using natural language or by Author, Title, ISBN and/or Date.

- The Daily Lists since July 1998.

- The Legal Advisor – a (chargeable) online service aimed at managers within local authorities and health authorities, bringing together primary and secondary sources of law, and offering advice and interpretation.

Acts of Parliament and Statutory Instruments are hosted on the HMSO site (see above and p 52).

The **Treasury Solicitor** provides legal services to most government departments and some other public bodies in England and Wales. It is one of the largest legal organisations in the UK.

Local government

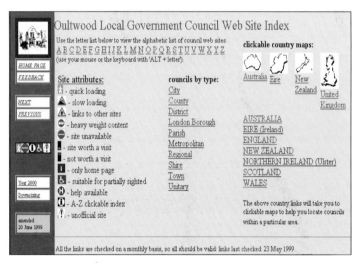

Most local autotrities are now online and new sites continue to appear. There are a few good jumping-off points from which they can be accessed:

- The **Oultwood Local Government Council website Index** covers UK and Irish (plus Australian and NZ) council websites. Entries are accessible by clickable maps or alphabetical lists and are coded using 'road signs' as to content, performance etc.

- The **CCTA Government Information Service** provides a comprehensive set of links.

- **Keith Edkins** maintains a useful site enabling you to find authorities using clickable maps or lists.

- **Brent Core IT** has links to all local government sites as well as a host of other information about local government.

Development of the Lord Chancellor's Department Website

by Mike Wicksteed

In the spring of 1997 someone remarked to me in passing that we had a pretty boring website. 'Boring?' I said, 'I didn't even know we had one.'

Eventually I tracked the website down to our IT branch and found it consisted of four documents. The Lord Chancellor's Department site had been up since late 1996, but no-one had bothered to tell the Communications directorate it had been established. It was boring.

Not a very positive start. But it set me thinking about the value of the internet as a communications tool. I concluded it could be a useful secondary information source.

Thought turned to jotting. I noted down a list of policy subject areas and general information topics that might be of interest to browsers. We would need to focus on policy information contained in consultation papers, press notices and speeches, rather than day-to-day operational matters, such as court judgments, forms or lists, the latter being the prerogative of the Court Service.

In turn this led me to think about who those browsers might be. I settled on three major groups: lawyers, legal academics and the media. There were obviously others: court users (being catered for by a team in the Court Service headquarters who, coincidentally, were just starting to develop their own website), students, civil servants working in adjacent policy areas and the general public, to name but a few.

But I knew nothing about the internet. To bone up on the subject I attended a seminar run by the Central Office of Information and was surprised at the burgeoning development of the internet throughout Government and Government agencies. I went on a three-day Civil Service College course called 'Hands-on Internet'. It provided an excellent basic training package on authoring, web page construction, security issues and general introductory background information.

The next question was how to physically develop the website. Flush with funds we weren't. So a Rolls Royce, tailor-made system, developed by a specialist website designer wasn't an option. However, we could afford to offer a summer vacation job to a student studying IT. If we could find such a person. Luckily we did - Stuart Tupper, doing post-graduate study at University College London.

With Stuart's help we quickly established a new interim site, providing a smattering of useful, easily authored material all of which was accessible directly from the front page.

In the meantime, with ease of navigation always to the fore, we were busy developing a modular website based on topic grid and sub-grids, reasoning that our basic concept must be able to cope with add-ons as the site expanded. We worked through a series of designs, some of which were very attractive but wouldn't necessarily present themselves to all browsers the same way.

In searching for excellence the route to achieving it always brought us back to ease of navigation as a priority. I had already accepted that with its relatively dry subject material the Department's website didn't need any bells or whistles. What readers would want was quick access to useful, accurate information; they certainly weren't going to be logging onto our site for entertainment.

'Simplicity' became our keyword. We settled on white background, black lettering and blue highlights. My only concession was an animated gif, a bit novel then, of a workman beavering away at a 'site under construction' sign. It was Stuart really.

Development continued throughout the rest of 1997 into early 1998.

The launch-date target was late January 1998, but what was the hurry? The interim site was proving a useful communications tool and, although wilting a bit under its design load, it would last a few more weeks. It was important to get the basics of the new site right at launch to avoid having to treat it as an interim in turn.

By now Stuart was back at university working for us in his spare time, labouring over document authoring and site development. In between periods of being a press officer I continued to seek out ideas for inclusion, visiting other Government and private sector websites in the UK and elsewhere, looking for what might work for us – and what wouldn't. No point in re-inventing the wheel.

I also came across the first edition of this publication, *Researching the Legal Web*, which, as a website novice, I found particularly stimulating. The highlighted pitfalls were particularly useful.

By mid-February 1998 we were almost there. But, before going live, I decided it would be sensible to ghost the site on the Central Computer and Telecommunications Agency's (CCTA) server to open it up to a selected group of experts, including Delia Venables and Nick Holmes, and potential users who could provide us with constructive criticism and feedback before we faced a wider audience. It was a good idea that paid dividends.

The new LCD site went live in March 1998. Over the intervening period the average number of 'unique' visits to our site has increased from about 400 per week to over 4,500. Many of our pages are now at the top of the CCTA's weekly statistical breakdown (see www.open.gov.uk/analog/stats.html).

In one important respect the website has evolved from being a secondary information tool and is now a vital necessity for many lawyers throughout England and Wales.

The introduction of the new Civil Procedure Rules early this year ushered in a new legal culture for our civil court system. Unlike the past rules, these new rules are not static; they are in a continual state of development. Our website offers lawyers and academics immediate access – free – to the rules when they appear on our website every month in a series of amendments and additions.

The quantum scale of this development, which started with the draft rules being placed on the website in late January 1999, took us by surprise. For a period it was a case of the tail wagging the dog. But we listened to the critical comments which were many and varied (in content and, sadly, tone) and worked hard to adjust the website to meet the needs of our users.

Luckily, the design of the site was sound enough to enable us to accommodate the increased requirements without our having to undertake a major restructuring exercise.

The Civil Procedure Rules are a direct result of the work undertaken by Lord Woolf, now Master of the Rolls, and his team in the mid-90s. It is mildly ironic that his 'Access to Justice' reports, accessible through the innovative University of Warwick website from 1995/96, were two of those first four documents on the LCD website.

And what does the future hold? In the short- to medium-term we will take part in a CCTA pilot initiative to provide our material in a format suitable for the visually impaired; we will also be exploring another CCTA initiative to 'group' similar topic websites. Generally we shall be looking at how best to provide an interactive service for our website's users.

In the longer term we will be seeking to widen access to the site by providing information in several languages. At present this is not practicable as software has yet to be developed for some scripts and the cost of translation is prohibitive: we were recently quoted in excess of £100,000 for the provision of a small subsection of our website in seven other languages – and in pdf only.

Finally, we are aware that technical web management, even on our relatively modest scale, is no longer a part-time job. In sporting terminology we need to 'turn professional'. A full-time LCD web manager is to be recruited who will also be tasked with developing an intranet for both LCD HQ and the Court Service.

The web thrives on evolution and our website will be no exception. The workman gif will be toiling away at the bottom of LCD's front page for some time to come.

Mike Wicksteed is Chief Press Officer at the Lord Chancellor's Department. Contact him at mwicksteed@lcdhq.gsi.gov.uk.

Parliaments

Links to Parliament sites are at www.infolaw.co.uk/ifl/govt.htm

Soon after the introduction of the historic legislation for the devolved parliaments, fresh new websites sprang up in anticipation of something to deliver! The new sites are all more attractive and sophisticated in design terms than the UK Parliament site – whether they are the better for it is difficult to tell at this stage.

Search the UK Parliament pages

1-10 of 1521 documents matching one or more words

Bills *(18 Feb 1999)*
Scottish Parliamentary Constituencies Bill [H.L.]
House of Lords Session 1998-99 Internet Publications Other Bills before Parliament Scottish Parliamentary Constituencies Bill [H L] This is the Scottish Parliamentary Constituencies Bill [H L], as introduced in the House of Lords on 17 February 1999. Scottish Parliamentary Constituencies Bill [H L] ARRANGEMENT OF CLAUSES Clause 1. Separate Boun.....

☐ Score: 100%, Matching *scottish parliament*

Bills *(08 Jul 1999)*
Finance Bill
Finance Bill - continued House of Lords back to previous text SCHEDULE 5 SCOTTISH PARLIAMENT AND DEVOLVED ASSEMBLIES. EXEMPTIONS AND RELIEFS Payments on dissolution, etc., or loss of office 1. For section 190 of the Taxes Act 1988 (exemption from charge as emoluments of certain payments made to members of Parliament and others) substitute- "Paymen.....

The results of a search for 'Scottish parliament' on the UK Parliament site

The **UK Parliament** at Westminster has had its own website (and its own domain) since mid-1996. The site has changed little since then, but nevertheless provides workmanlike access to the Houses' information and publications, including Hansard, Bills befor Parliament, Select Committee publications, the Weekly Information Bulletin and a Register of Lords Interests.

There is a useful extensive alphabetical index to the site and you can also search the site, first selecting from a range of documents (Bills, Commons Hansards etc or All). Searches are either in your own words (free text) or by the name of an individual (speaker). You can also specifically include a Parliamentary Question number in your search, and optionally specify a date range.

Further details of the content of the site are under 'Parliamentary proceedings' on p 54, and for House of Lords judgments see p 55.

The business of the new **Scottish Parliament** can be tracked using a What's Happening section on the site. Other sections of the site cover Members of the Scottish Parliament (MSPs), Agenda and Decisions, Official Report, Young People and Teachers and the Parliament Buildings. See further Chapter 11.

The **Northern Ireland Assembly** site provides pages for What's New, General Information about the Assembly, Publications, Committees, the Assembly Commission and a Register of Members' Interests.

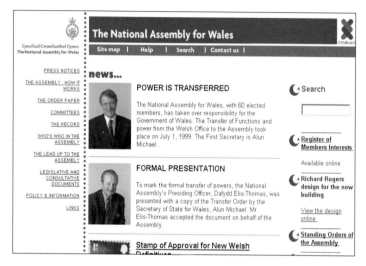

The **Welsh Assembly** site is clearly laid out, giving access to Press Notices, How it Works, the Order Paper, Committees, the Record of Proceedings, Who's Who, the Lead up to the Assembly, Legislative and Consultative Documents and useful Links. There is also a Search facility.

Europarl is the multi-lingual webserver of the European Parliament Activities, including extensive information divided into the following categories: ABC (overview, basic information and addresses), Activities, Press, and References, including a searchable database of Treaties and Basic Documents and Official Journals.

The Courts

Links to court service sites are at www.infolaw.co.uk/ifl/govt.htm

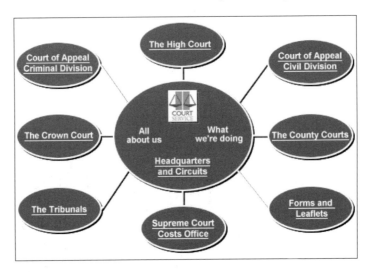

The **Court Service**, which is an executive agency of the Lord Chancellor's Department, provides administrative support to a number of courts and tribunals, including the High Court, the Crown Court and the county courts. Whilst the outcome of cases coming before the courts and tribunals is determined by a judge or judicial officer, much of the supporting administrative work is carried out by the staff of the Court Service.

The pages give a diagrammatic representation of the court structure with links from each branch to selected Judgments, Daily Lists and Practice Directions relating to that court. There are also links where appropriate to external sites such as the Immigration Appellate Authority.

The County Court section lists all the courts and addresses and provides an index to determine which court has geographical jurisdiction for a particular parish within England and Wales.

The Forms and Leaflets pages include well indexed sets of many court forms, including the new civil procedure forms, in Adobe pdf format. As to forms on the web, see further p 59.

As to the provision of judgments on the web, see p 55; and as to court practice and procedure, see p 57.

The **Scottish Courts Website** is described in Chapter 11.

The **Northern Ireland Court Service** provides a handful of documents online.

Professional Bodies

Links to professional bodies' sites are at www.venables.co.uk/legal/sites2.htm#gateways and www.infolaw.co.uk/ifl/assoc.htm

The Law Society

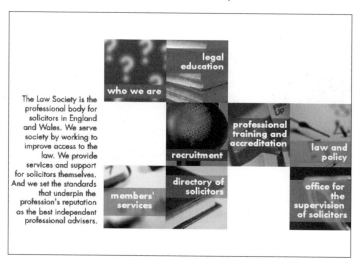

The Law Society is the professional body for solicitors in England and Wales. We serve society by working to improve access to the law. We provide services and support for solicitors themselves. And we set the standards that underpin the profession's reputation as the best independent professional advisers.

who we are — legal education — professional training and accreditation — law and policy — recruitment — directory of solicitors — members' services — office for the supervision of solicitors

The Law Society set up one of the first legal websites in 1995 and has been developing it steadily ever since. It is now very impressive and will doubtless play an increasing role in the life of the Society over the next few years.

The Society has to cater to several different groups: it is visited frequently by members of the public, looking for information (typically about how to become a solicitor or looking for information on the English legal system), by solicitors themselves, accessing the information produced by the Society, and by members of the public wanting to complain. It has to meet the expectations of all these.

The site provides information about the sections and work of the Society, including press releases, consultations, proposals and general news. There is a comprehensive list of members' services, a useful set of links to legal resources on the web and an online version of the *Law Society's Gazette* (see further p 67).

The Directory of Solicitors is not yet online but will be at some point.

The Law Society of Scotland

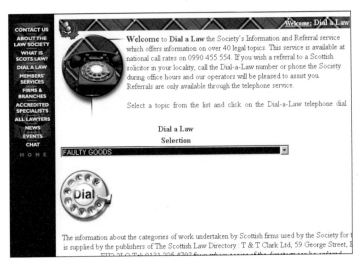

The **Law Society of Scotland** is a more recent arrival on the web than the English Law Society but it is making great efforts to make up for lost time. In some areas it is ahead of its southern cousin.

For example, the full directory of Scottish Solicitors is already available in a fully searchable form and there is a comprehensive system available for referring members of the public to a solicitor specialising in their required area of law, in their locality.

There is also a Dial a Law facility where the viewer chooses an area of law from 40 available topics and is then provided with useful background on the topic as well as being invited to ring in for a referral to a Scottish solicitor.

There is also information on Scots History and Law, the Structure of the Courts, information on legal training, information on members' services and current news from the Society.

There is also a full list of events and courses put on by the Society and another innovative feature not yet available on the English Law Society site – a chat section open only to members of the Society.

The Law Society of Ireland

The Law Society is the educational, representative and regulatory body of the solicitors' profession in Ireland. The Law Society was established in 1773 and now exercises statutory functions under the Solicitors Acts 1954-1994 in relation to the education, admission, enrolment, discipline and regulation of the solicitors' profession.

The Society works to improve access to the law generally and also provides representation, services and support for solicitors themselves.

The Society also deals with complaints from the public about members of the profession and administers a statutory compensation fund.

There are currently over 5,000 solicitors practising in Ireland. The content of this Site provides an overview of the work of the solicitors' profession and of The Law Society.

Please contact the webmaster **Claire O'Sullivan**, tel:01 672 4829

Practice provides an overview of the work of the Council of The Law Society and its various professional committees. It also includes details of practice notes issued by The Law Society.

Profile includes useful contact names of Law Society personnel and an outline of the rich history of the Society and its historic premises at Blackhall Place.

Member Services details the full range of Law Society services available to solicitors.

What's new provides details of Society publications, recruitment, forthcoming seminars and the current continuing legal education programme.

Education provides details on becoming an apprentice and qualifying as a solicitor in Ireland.

Gazette is the award winning journal of the Law Society and includes features and articles on issues of legal interest.

Links provide a guide to useful internet sites of interest to legal practitioners.

Launched relatively recently, in early 1999, the **Law Society of Ireland** site has been able to burst, fully formed, upon the legal community in Ireland. Whilst not attempting to do anything really difficult (there is no directory of solicitors, no searching capabilities, no referral services and no chat sections) the site is nevertheless filled with useful information and is kept up to date.

The main contents of the site can be seen from the picture above. An additional feature of the What's New section is a series of current news items relating to Government publications and press releases, European initiatives (such as the euro changeover process) and Law Society papers and consultations. This appears to be a useful current awareness resource.

The Bar Council

The General Council Of The Bar®

...to provide positive contributions to the furtherance of justice
with due regard to the interests of the profession...

Access To Excellence

B arristers of England and Wales are high quality, highly competitive specialist advocates, experts in the conduct of the client's case at trial. For advocacy, advice or arbitration in matters involving English or European law the English Bar is a rich source of talent, expertise and specialisation.

The Role Of The Specialist

Advocacy Barristers appear in most major cases in the English courts. Their unrivalled fund of experience is available to foreign lawyers and other professionals, governments, companies and individual clients* around the world. Where litigation takes place outside England and Wales, the barrister may be appointed direct. Where the case is pursued in the English courts, a solicitor is used to instruct the barrister.

The **Bar Council** site seems to be designed as much for the general public as for barristers themselves. There is a considerable amount of information provided about the history of the bar and about the responsibilities and skills involved in practising as a barrister.

The 'only official directory of UK chambers' can be accessed from the site; this is a joint venture between Sweet & Maxwell (formerly FT Law & Tax) and the Bar Council. You can search by name, specialism, area and even language spoken.

Another part of the site covers education and training, both in the process of becoming a barrister, and also on the topic of Continuing Professional Development. This section includes a discussion group and a set of links.

There is a notice board covering speeches, press releases and reports, but it does not seem to be updated very often – there are only four entries for the last year!

The Institute of Legal Executives

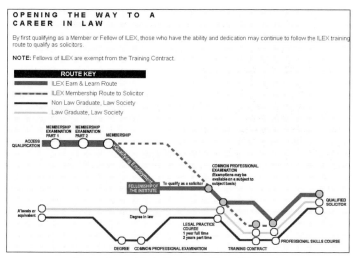

OPENING THE WAY TO A CAREER IN LAW

By first qualifying as a Member or Fellow of ILEX, those who have the ability and dedication may continue to follow the ILEX training route to qualify as solicitors.

NOTE: Fellows of ILEX are exempt from the Training Contract.

Getting there with the Institute of Legal Executives

The **Institute of Legal Executives** (ILEX) is the professional body representing over 23,000 legal executives and trainee legal executives.

A key role of the body is in education. The ILEX training route leads to a recognised and much sought after qualification in law and legal practice. Most trainees are in full-time employment and study part-time by day release or evening classes, or by taking an ILEX Tutorial College (ITC) home study course – combining both study and examination with practical experience.

The various routes to a career in the law are described and also charted, as seen above – is that all clear then?

A list of Colleges is given for the courses available, with full contact details.

There are a number of other topics covered on the site, including the process of Law Reform, and of new Rights of Audience.

The Society for Computers and Law

The SCL e-mag

The **Society for Computers and Law** plays an important role in the life of lawyers interested in IT, both concerning the use of IT for lawyers and in the law relating to IT.

The main features of the site are as follows:

- SCL Diary contains information about current meetings for all groups of the society.

- SCL e-mag is the online version of the SCL journal *Computers & Law*. This is an excellent publication with serious and well informed articles and is well worth viewing on a regular basis.

- SCL Groups is a set of links to websites of individual area groups and interest groups. The structure is set up for all groups to have an entry but only about half the groups have taken on this task, so far.

- SCL Buzzboard is intended to contain current interesting news items, including feedback from members, but it has to be said that, so far, this page has not really taken off.

- SCL Resources is a useful set of links to legal resources in the UK and worldwide.

Firms of Solicitors

Links to law firm websites are at www.venables.co.uk/legal/firms.htm and www.infolaw.co.uk/ifl/lawyers.htm

There are around 500 firms of Solicitors in England and Wales with websites, 70 in Scotland, a handful in Northern Ireland and around 40 in the Republic of Ireland. These vary from very large firms to sole practitioners. Here are some examples.

A large firm

CLIFFORD CHANCE
Clifford Chance is a leading international law firm that provides comprehensive advice on a wide range of financial, corporate, commercial and dispute resolution matters.
We provide a uniquely integrated service from our network of offices in all major business and financial centres around the world.

FIND OUT ABOUT THE FIRM

INTERNATIONAL REACH worldwide network of offices	**PRESS OFFICE** for the latest news
WIDE RANGE OF EXPERIENCE practice areas capabilities specialist groups partners biographies and contacts	**PUBLICATIONS** our publications in print **CAREER** for recruitment information
WHAT'S NEW recent additions to the site	**SEARCH** our website

In Europe Clifford Chance is based in Amsterdam, Barcelona, Brussels, Budapest, Düsseldorf, Frankfurt, London, Madrid, Milan, Moscow, Padua, Paris, Prague, Rome and Warsaw. We have relationships with correspondent firms in all the other European capital cities.

Outside Europe, Clifford Chance has offices in Bangkok, Dubai, Hong Kong, Hanoi, Ho Chi Minh City, New York, São Paulo, Singapore, Shanghai, Tokyo, and Washington D.C.

The **Clifford Chance** site may be unexciting to look at, but it is a truly massive site with a great deal of information.

For example, when this picture was taken, the online newsletters, all dated within the preceding few months, included: Russia and the other States of the CIS, Asian Financial Markets Newsletter, China News in Brief, Employment News in Brief, Private Finance Initiative, Europe in Prospect, China Banking News, Securities and Derivatives, European Financial Markets, Legal Risk in the Financial Sector, International Investment Funds Review, Insurance Review and Asian M&A

Some of the largest firms, including Clifford Chance and Linklaters, are offering legal advice online. This is covered further in Chapter 8.

Medium sized firms with special expertise

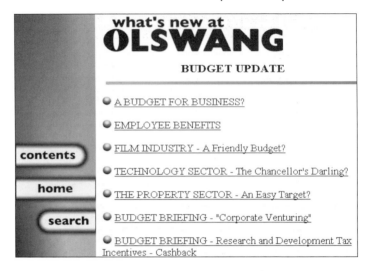

It does not follow that larger firms have the better pages: indeed, it is sometimes easier for a medium sized firm, with a simple message and a human face, to produce a lively and interesting website than a large corporate style firm.

The **Olswang** site, for example, offers briefings in various topics, and also provides details of its media and entertainment business clients (a very impressive list) and some lighthearted material about not being just grey suits.

Tarlo Lyons, another firm concentrating on media, entertainment and IT, also has a striking site. They concentrate on the Year 2000 problem, EMU, and various papers on domain names and defamation in cyberspace. The overall impression is given of a high tech firm providing immediate and clear information on IT topics.

Other IT and media-oriented firms, including Fox Williams, Bird & Bird and Jeffrey Green Russell. All provide briefings, online newsletters and visually interesting features.

Major provincial firms

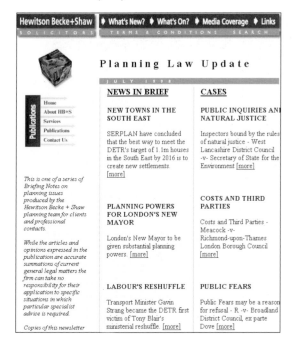

Hewitson Becke & Shaw, in Cambridgeshire opens its site with a friendly set of faces but moves on to present a series of newsletters online in an attractive format on a whole series of business and commercial topics. The firm itself is well covered in these newsletters – well, the whole purpose of any firm's website is to present themselves well, so that does seem a reasonable approach.

The series of Newsletters available includes Business Briefing, Commercial Property Review, Debt Services, Employment Law Review, Intellectual Property Review, Private Client & Investor Review, Construction Law Update and Planning Law Update.

The impression is given of a solid regional firm with a wide expertise.

Smaller firms

Terry & Co., UK Solicitors

We are UK solicitors who specialise in advising general members of the public and small businesses. The topics below are illustrative rather than exhaustive. In practice, for example, a small business might be more interested in contracts of employment, the formation of a limited company, taking a lease on commercial premises etc so please do not hesitate to contact us if your particular query is not specifically mentioned.

About Us	Accidents	Children - Contact, Maintenance etc	Cohabitees
Consumer Law	Conveyancing	Elderly - particular problems	Gay
Legal Aid	Litigation	Matrimonial & Divorce	Landlord & Tenant
Wills & Probate	Others?	Subject Index - More detailed information	Comments?

Some of the small firms – the ones with one or more partners who really believe in the future of the web for bringing in clients and indeed carrying out the work online – have provided some surprises and some innovations. For example, **Kaye Tesler & Co** carries out several types of forms-based work on the web, and some niche firms can make particularly good marketing presentations. Some of these firms are described in Chapter 8, Lawyers Doing Business on the Web.

A site which really speaks for itself is **Terry & Co** (above).

Quite a few firms have included information on their sites which cover particular legal topics and indeed it is possible to learn a great deal from these presentations.

A selected list of these firms, with the information they are presenting grouped by category (accidents, benefits, consumer issues etc), is given at www.venables.co.uk/legal/individ.htm. Another list is maintained of the information offered on commercial topics (generally provided by the larger firms) at www.venables.co.uk/legal/commerce.htm.

Scottish firms

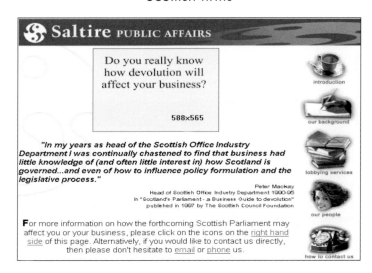

Scottish firms have always been quite advanced and early on the web – perhaps they see the web as an opportunity to be in the centre of things even if their physical location is not so central.

Now, with the Parliament in Scotland, Scottish firms are taking account of some new opportunities. For example, one major firm, **Shepherd & Wedderburn**, has set up a new legal lobbying organisation called **Saltire Public Affairs** and devoted a substantial part of the overall website to the presentation of this topic.

Other firms providing information on the new Parliament and how it will operate include **Robson Mclean**, **Brodies** and **McGrigor Donald**.

Another area where Scotland is ahead of other areas of the UK is in the presentation of information on property (many firms are also Estate Agents). Firms with interesting presentations on property, including pictures and generally the ability to ask for more information, either as a pdf file or in the mail, include **South Forrest**, **Brodies** and **Georgesons**.

Overall, the standard is high. Firms with good websites (not an exhaustive list) include Biggart Baillie, Bishop and Robertson-Chalmers, Boyds, Brodies, Bird Semple, Georgesons, Gillespie Gifford & Brown, Henderson Boyd Jackson, Mcgrigor Donald, MacRoberts, Maclay Murray & Spens, South Forrest and Thorntons.

Irish Firms

Many Irish firms' websites are well constructed and full of useful information. Here are just a few of the most interesting ones.

William Fry – Dublin. This is an example of a major firm really putting effort into its website and providing legal news and other useful information. There is a wide variety of publications placed on line, mainly on business and commercial topics, including an ongoing set of notes on e-commerce with respect to Ireland in particular.

A & L Goodbody – Dublin. An impressive site with a great deal of information intended for potential clients. Part of the site is also available in French and also German. There is a section on Current Legal News covering such topics as Internet Law (for example, Internet Regulation in Ireland), Y2K, and EMU, and there is a major section on setting up business in Ireland, including geographic, legal, regulatory and financial information.

Frank Lanigan Malcomson & Law – Carlow and Dublin. This is an example of a small firm which knows what it is doing – pitching for private client work and particularly looking for work involving Hepatitis B claims work. This site would come up in search engines (extensive use is made of meta-tags) and it has apparently already brought in some useful work.

McCann FitzGerald – Dublin. Billing itself as one of Ireland's largest firms, this site provides a series of legal briefings on different topics (employment, energy, EU legislation, to take a few from the middle of the list). There is also a section on Ireland as a business location and a number of rather meaty legal briefings.

Law Firm Groups

Links to law firm group websites are at www.venables.co.uk/legal/firmgrou.htm and www.infolaw.co.uk/ifl/lawyers.htm

There are a considerable number of law firm groups, some based just in the UK and some covering firms in several countries, notably across Europe. These websites generally have a rather heavy and 'corporate' feel, probably being the product of a committee decision rather than a few individuals' personal enthusiasm.

Here are the ones known to us at present. The descriptions draw mainly from the words used by the groups themselves.

The **Association of Commercial Lawyers International** (ACL International) is a network of 38 firms comprising over 800 lawyers. Member firms around the world offer advice and a global service to clients. ACL offers clients the benefits of local representation in a foreign jurisdiction and local knowledge of cross-border transactions.

CMS is a transnational legal services organisation, involving (in the UK) Cameron McKenna, which now calls itself **CMS Cameron McKenna**. The site says: 'As one of the world's largest legal groups, CMS has the resources and experience to advise on cross-border transactions and address multi-jurisdictional legal issues, backed up by strong domestic practices.'

Eurojuris International is a grouping of over 720 law firms in 18 countries throughout Europe and Scandinavia and covering 650 different cities/locations. The group is composed of 18 national Associations, bringing together medium-sized law firms from each country.

Euro-Link for Lawyers is one of the largest international legal networks and legal associations in the world. It acts as a facilitator of international legal services bringing together the combined strengths of over 50 commercial legal practices and law firms, over 425 partners and 65 offices world-wide.

The **European Law Firm** is a grouping of EU law firms and non-EU associate members offering legal services throughout the European Union, and across its internal and external frontiers. It brings together some 250 lawyers practising in all areas of business law.

The **Euro-American Lawyers Group** is an International Association of law firms in the US and Europe.

IAG International is a multi-disciplinary group, including lawyers, accountants, tax advisors, real estate advisors, fiduciaries and others. The group is designed for the business person or private individual with cross border transactions or investments to execute or manage.

The **International Bar Association**, founded in 1947, is the world's largest international organisation of Law Societies, Bar Associations and individual lawyers engaged in international law. It is composed of over 18,000 individual lawyer members in 183 countries and 173 Law Societies and Bar Associations together representing more than 2.5 million lawyers.

Interleges, the International Association of independent law firms, has offices across the countries of the European Union, Eastern Europe, North America, the Middle East and in other key commercial regions of the world.

The **International Network of Independent Lawyers** provides access to legal services across frontiers, throughout Europe, Asia and the Middle East.

Lawnet is a major grouping of independent firms in many locations throughout the United Kingdom, the Republic of Ireland and the Channel Islands.

Logos is a network of independent law firms in Europe. With one law firm in each of the 12 countries of the European Union and contacts in the other three, Logos can assist any business or law firm around the world that needs legal support in Europe.

Mackrell International is a world wide association of 40 independent law firms created to meet the increasingly complex and varied needs of clients throughout the world, and to respond to the challenges of the international and commercial market.

The **Motor Accident Solicitors Society** (MASS) is an association of solicitors' firms with experience and expertise in the handling of motor accident claims. Member firms are located throughout the UK. The site provides a list of firms which are part of MASS and which can be searched by region.

The **National Solicitors Network** is a network of independent solicitors' practices with over 500 member offices throughout England and Wales which is setting new standards in the provision of high quality, reasonably priced services.

The **Solicitors Pro Bono Group** aims to encourage and assist firms to provide free legal services where other means of finance are not available. The site is hosted on the Society for Computers and Law site.

Barristers

Links to barristers' websites are at www.venables.co.uk/legal/bar.htm and www.infolaw.co.uk/ifl/lawyers.htm

There are around 90 chambers with their own websites and a handful of individual barristers. Sites broadly fall into the following categories:

- Brochure sites which have taken the printed material and converted it to a website format. Some of these are well designed and informative even though usually, it has to be said, a trifle unexciting.

- Sites which are setting up centres of expertise in particular areas of law. By becoming well known for providing useful (free) information, they hope to become associated in peoples' minds with that particular type of work.

- Individual barristers' sites, where (presumably) their chambers are not yet ready to adopt the internet culture, and where the barrister is exploring the possibilities on a personal basis in the meantime.

Brochure sites

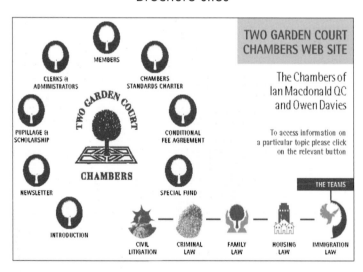

2 Garden Court is an attractive example of a brochure site. This set was founded with a strong commitment to the legal aid system and with a particular emphasis upon criminal defence and civil rights. There are 54 full members including four QC's and, now, a wide range of work.

Centres of expertise

Following are some of the chambers which are working to become recognised centres of expertise:

One Crown Office Row hosts an ongoing analysis of the Human Rights Act with references to leading cases in this country and a digest of Strasbourg case law.

Exchange Chambers, based in Liverpool, offer a number of articles on personal injury cases.

Gray's Inn is a specialist tax advice and tax appeal litigation chambers. There are online digests of recent tax cases in which members have appeared, with full transcripts in some cases. There are also links to other tax sites, world wide.

HARDWICKE BUILDING
PropertyGroup

PROPERTY GROUP HELPLINE
020 7691 0022
9:00AM TO 5:30PM MON-FRI

April 1999 | May 1999 | June 1999 | July 1999

Hardwicke Building Home
Front Page
Get the big picture
News
What's going on
In Depth
Property topics in detail
Did You See?
Recent cases
Events
Conferences, seminars
Up Close
Meet the group members
Contact Us
How to reach us

Cases galore!
A bumper crop of recent cases, particularly Landlord & Tenant, feature in this months Did You See? section.

Elsewhere we take a look at recent case involving the summary possession of land against trespassers. The judgment of the widely reported case of Dutton v Manchester Airport plc substantially broadens the class of claimants who may seek summary possession and that applications under Part II of C.24 (Interim Possession Orders) require the claimant to have an immediate right to possession and to have had "such a right throughout the period of unlawful occupation complained of".

Last month we ran a Property & Family Breakdown seminar for a capacity audience. Chaired by Nicholas Stewart QC, the seminar covered areas including Trusts of Land, Schedule 1 of the Children Act and Insolvency of One Family Member. If you could not make the

Welcome
The Hardwicke Building Property Group aims to keep you up to date with what is going on in property law and this service compliments and extends the information already available through our printed newsletter.

Here you will find more news, in depth articles, case listings, details about the property group itself and access to individual CVs

We hope you find this service useful and we welcome any suggestions and feedback you may have. Please address any comments to:
editor@hardwicke.co.uk.

Hardwicke Buildings specialises in civil, commercial, crime and family law and particularly in professional negligence, landlord and tenant and international child abduction. There is a Property Group Newsletter on the site with news, developments and cases; you can register to receive notification of new issues.

11 Kings Bench Walk Publishes articles written by members of chambers with commentary on current cases, particularly in the area of employment law, commercial law and European law.

Lancaster Buildings Northern Intellectual Property Chambers provides a number of articles including a commentary on the new Civil Procedures Rules.

1 Mitre Court Buildings is a specialist family law chambers. There is a news section which provides 'a quick look at some recent interesting family law cases'. There are also a number of calculators for tax and benefits and a set of links to family law sites.

11 New Square – another tax-based site – includes articles on tax law and some links to other websites relating to tax issues.

2 Temple Gardens has made a name for itself by providing the first substantial commentary and interpretation of the new Civil Procedures Rules on the web and has linked this activity with a major marketing effort. There is more on this topic in the Chapter 'Lawyers Doing Business on the Web'.

Individual barristers

Daniel Barnett, of 2 Gray's Inn Chambers, is a specialist in employment law and has set up an employment law mailing list. There is information about how to join this on his website. He also offers news flashes and a set of links in employment law.

Tony Bingham, of 3 Paper Buildings, is a construction barrister, arbitrator, adjudicator and columnist for *Building Magazine*. The site also contains information about the building and construction industry, together with building and construction law, and a good set of links in these areas.

Roger Horne, of 11 New Square, Lincoln's Inn, has developed an index of cases, and cases referred to, in House of Lords judgments. (The judgments published on the House of Lords' site are completely without indexing or cross referencing of any kind, which makes them of very limited use). The index provides an example of what could be done in law reporting on the web. He also provides a cross-referenced version of the new Civil Procedure Rules.

Jonathan S Schwarz, of 3 Temple Gardens, specialises in international taxation. He is also admitted to the Bar in South Africa and Canada and his website contains several very detailed papers on transfer pricing.

Gary Webber, at 33 Bedford Row, specialises in property law, and is author of books on possession actions. His site includes a substantial paper on standard possession claims in the county court under the CPR and another on mortgage possession claims in the High Court and the county court.

Laurie West-Knights of 4 Paper Buildings, specialises in commercial contract litigation including that relating to computers. He maintains an excellent set of links to legal material on his page, called LawOnLine, which is probably the most up to date and well researched set of links anywhere on the web to 'What there is now in terms of free access to real, primary law'. He also has a section of commentary on the Civil Procedure Rules.

Irish Barristers

Links to Irish barristers are at www.venables.co.uk/legal/barirel.htm

Until very recently, there was only one Irish barrister with a website – **Kieron Wood**. When he set up his site, in 1997, this was considered to be touting and there were complaints laid against him by the professional practices committee of the Bar Council. However, the Bar Council is currently reconsidering its position on this and now there are several barristers with websites although all the sites are safely on the side of 'information providing' rather than self promotion.

Kieron provides information on Defamation Law, the Divorce Act (simplified), Divorce Paperwork, Family Law Statutes, Wills, Irish Legal Terminology and a list of Irish Barristers with phone numbers.

See also his article on Irish Legal Resources, Chapter 12.

Twinkle Egan provides a centralised European Convention causebook and judgment registry database.

Gillian Kelly has a series of four papers on post traumatic stress disorder as a recognizable psychiatric illness in the light of the 1995 Irish Supreme Court judgment in *Kelly v Hennessy*.

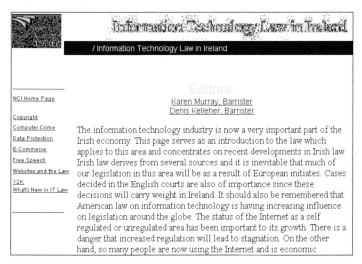

Denis Kelleher and Karen Murray provide information on information technology law, hosted by the National College of Industrial Relations. The site covers copyright, computer crime, data protection, e-commerce, Y2K and what's new in IT law.

Fergus O'Rourke covers the topic of utmost good faith (uberrima fides) and insurance law generally, in an Irish (and UK) context.

Associations of Individual Lawyers

Links to lawyer association websites are at www.venables.co.uk/legal/groups.htm and www.infolaw.co.uk/ifl/assoc.htm

The professional associations, such as the Law Societies and the Bar Council, have already been covered under Professional Bodies above, p 27. This section covers the smaller and more specialist associations. Many of these are run by enthusiastic members of the group concerned and there is an element of volatility about these; it is of interest that, of the five such associations described in the first edition of this book, only two now remain. Probably, a number of the ones below, particularly the ones hosted on the free space of some of the internet service providers, will suffer a similar fate!

Despite the volatility, the number of legal groups and associations with a website has grown rapidly over the last two years and quite a number of these have their own domain name and a professional looking appearance. Some are based on Universities' web servers and others are hosted on the site of a larger firm or organisation.

Here are the main associations that we know of. The descriptions are drawn largely from the groups' own web pages.

The **Association of Child Abuse Lawyers** provides practical support for lawyers and other professionals working for adults and children who have been abused. The assocation – and the site – is developing rapidly and now provides a useful news section, with frequent updates, as well as a newsletter with longer articles and a central record of group actions against care homes. The group is urgently seeking new members, funds and energies.

The **Association of Law Teachers**, hosted at the University of Warwick, aims to further the study, understanding and reform of educational aspects of law, to represent members views on the teaching of law, and to support and encourage activities which will be of use and benefit to law teachers.

The **Association of Personal Injury Lawyers** is dedicated to improving the service provided to victims of accident and medical negligence. Over 4,000 solicitors and barristers work with the Association to fight for law reform to improve access to justice.

The **Bar Association for Local Government and the Public Service** is a direct successor of the Society of Local Government Barristers, which had been in existence since about 1945, and of the Bar Association for Local Government, which had been formed in 1977. Membership is open to all barristers employed in Local Government and the Public Sector (including those in the civil service and in the armed forces) and bar students.

The **British & Irish Legal Education Technology Association** (BILETA) was formed in 1986 with the primary objective of promoting technology in legal education throughout the United Kingdom and Ireland. It is hosted on Warwick University's site.

The **British and Irish Association of Law Librarians** (BIALL) was formed in 1969 to represent effectively the interests of all those involved in law librarianship.

The **British-Italian Law Association** is designed to provide mutual interest and information for lawyers in the two countries.

Clarity is the International Movement for Plain Legal Language, hosted by Solicitors Adler & Adler. There is a journal, a set of seminars, and occasional meetings.

The **Discrimination Law Association** aims 'to promote and improve the giving of advice to, and representation of, and support to complainants of discrimination, harassment or abuse on such grounds as race, gender, religion, disability, sexual orientation, age, health status, political opinion, marital or family status and trade union affiliation or activity.' There is also a useful set of links to organisations in this general area.

The **Employed and Non-Practising Bar Association** campaigns for rights for non-practising barristers. There is information about the group and its campaigns and a free newsletter.

Euro-Lex International is non-profit organisation of legal practitioners in any field and from any country, desiring to study the problems derived from the application of International Law and Business Law.

The **Family Mediators Association** offers trained mediators to help all couples facing separation or divorce to reach decisions about dealing with children, property and finance. They train and support Family Mediators, and, as one of the founder members of the UK College of Family Mediation, set and monitor standards in Family Mediation.

The **Forum of Insurance Lawyers** (FOIL) 'is not a mouth-piece for the insurance industry: it is a mouthpiece for all lawyers, solicitors and legal executives, who act for insurance companies. Where there is a conflict of view between insurers and their legal professionals then it is FOIL's job to represent the interests of the lawyers concerned'.

The **Fungible Trust** provides a focus for the study and practice of Fungible Trusts, to enable any competent practitioner to create and use Fungible Trusts. It is hoped that the site will eventually contain all the necessary forms and precedents for Fungible Trusts along with a wide range of articles and examples.

The **Immigration Law Practitioners' Association** is the UK's professional association of lawyers and academics practising in or concerned about immigration, asylum and nationality law. Its membership currently stands at 820. Membership is by application supported by two references and subject to an annual membership fee. It is only open to persons subject to a professional disciplinary body.

The **Law Management Section** of the Law Society is a forum for the exchange of the latest ideas and information across the spectrum of management disciplines. It is open to all solicitors and those involved in law firm management. The group provides a newsletter, seminars and discounts on various publications and intends to be a useful source of information generally.

The **Legal Action Group** (LAG) is the national, independent charity which campaigns for equal access to justice for all members of society and supports lawyers who share that aim. The group is now 25 years old.

The **Lawyers' Christian Fellowship** was originally founded in 1852, in London, as the Lawyers' Prayer Union. Now it has grown to become a national organisation with around 1,300 members at every stage of the legal profession. There is a special section for students and a set of links to other organisations relating both to legal and to religious sites.

The **Lawyers Flying Association** is the UK group of those involved with the legal profession who share a common enthusiasm for aviation in general and private flying in particular. It has just celebrated its tenth anniversary.

The **National Association of Paralegals** caters for unadmitted support staff in Solicitors' offices. They provide a professional career progression with qualifications obtained through examinations and assessment (courses run by FE colleges throughout the country) and also put on short vocational courses, seminars and workshops.

The **Notaries' Society** is the representative body for the 900 or so Notaries Public practising in England and Wales outside Central London.

The **Pan-European Organisation of Personal Injury Lawyers** (PEOPIL) aims to develop co-operation and networking of personal injury lawyers within Europe and to promote access to the legal system for consumers suffering personal injury. It is based on APIL as well as other individual lawyers across Europe.

The **Oxford Liberty Group**, a local group of Liberty (National Council for Civil Liberties), features a range of information and will shortly include a library of Liberty's briefings on legal developments impinging on civil liberties. A briefing on the incorporation of the ECHR is available. Contacts for other branches are given, with web links if available. The group is hosted by Oxford University.

The **Scottish Law Agents Society** is a voluntary society of Scottish lawyers, active since 1884.

The **Society of Construction Law** is a group of over 700 members from all sectors of the construction industry. There is a newsletter, information about events and links to construction-related websites.

The **Society of Trust and Estate Practitioners** (STEP) is the Professional body for the trust and estate profession in the UK and worldwide. STEP members come from the legal, accountancy, corporate trust, banking, insurance and related professions, and are involved at senior level in the planning, creation, management of and accounting for trusts and estates, executorship administration, and related taxes.

SolCare gives health support and advice for Solicitors on alcohol problems, depression, stress and drugs. There is a discussion of how to identify fellow professionals who are addicted to alcohol or drugs, how to help them to come to terms with their condition and how to help them to return to practice following treatment. There are also links to other articles on these topics.

The **Socio-Legal Studies Association**, hosted by Westminster University, is dedicated to improving the quality of and facilities for socio-legal research.

The **Sole Practitioners Group of the Law Society** (4,800 members) has useful information about the group and future events and also responses to the SIF developments and Legal Aid Board initiatives. Local groups are beginning to set up their own pages, with Yorkshire in the lead.

The **Solicitors Family Law Association** (SFLA) represents over 4,000 solicitors who specialise in divorce and family issues. They are committed to adopting a conciliatory approach to family breakdown.

The **Solicitors Pro Bono Group** describes its aims and activities and there is a special area for members. The site is hosted on the Society for Computers and Law site.

The **Trainee Solicitors Group** is a national organisation which represents students of law during their CPE and LPC, and trainee solicitors during their training contracts through to the end of their first year of admission as a solicitor. It has approximately 20,000 members.

The **UK Environmental Law Association** is the national association for those involved in the practice, study or formulation of Environmental Law. It has amongst its aims: to collate and disseminate information relating to environmental law; and to identify, review, advise and comment on issues of environmental law and its application.

Mackrell International
An International Association of Law Firms
MACKRELL
INTERNATIONAL
An International
Association of
Independent Law Firms
GLOBAL COVERAGE
LOCAL EXPERTISE
About
Companies
Papers
Guest Book
Search
Contents
Americas
Europe / Africa
Asia / Australia
Members by Company Name
About Mackrell
Papers
Please Sign Our Guest Book
Search
Table of Contents

Chapter 3

What's on the Legal Web

Contents

This chapter describes in some detail the wide range of legal materials, information and other services available for the UK lawyer on the web. Except where otherwise indicated, there is generally free access to the materials described here. Chapter 4 reviews the information services provided by the commercial law publishers. There are many free services available on these sites, but the more substantial, 'premium' services are generally available only on subscription. Chapter 5 summarises many other useful sites providing resources for specific areas of law and practice.

Legislation

www.legislation.hmso.gov.uk

HMSO's Legislation website gives access to the full texts of Acts published since January 1996, plus the Data Protection Act 1984, the Criminal Appeal Act 1995 and the Disability Discrimination Act 1995; explanatory notes of Acts from 1999 and summaries of a wide range of earlier Acts comprising long title, arrangement of sections, ISBN, page content and price. The full texts of all Statutory Instruments passed from January 1997 are also published.

The legislation home page now gives access to four libraries: UK Legislation (pictured above) and one for each of the three new legislatures.

HMSO's aim is 'to publish these documents on the internet simultaneously or at least within 24 hours of their publication in printed from. However, any document which is especially complex in terms of its size or its typography may take longer to prepare.'

You can search across the legislation databases using the Muscat search engine which accommodates natural language search terms, such as 'Statutes on companies published in 1998'.

It is worth noting that the Acts appear as originally passed by Parliament, ie unamended, and with no indication of which sections are in force. These are fairly basic deficiencies both for the lawyer and for the unsuspecting layman who takes the text to be a statement of the current law – a deficiency addressed by the Statute Law Database (see below).

The Acts are accessed by year from an alphabetical list by title. The arrangement of sections of each Act is presented, and each section title provides a link to the text of that section. Sections are presented in chunks, generally corresponding to Parts or Chapters of the Act, so that one can scroll up and down across contiguous sections. Links are provided at the top and bottom of each chunk to return to the previous chunk or continue to the next. Hypertext links to cross-referenced sections are, however, *not* provided.

The presentation of SIs is similar to that of the Acts, though each SI is generally presented complete on one web page, and hypertext links to footnotes (giving numbers of, but not links to, cross-referenced Acts and SIs) are provided.

The SIs are listed by year and number, so if you don't know the SI number, you will need to find the SI using the HMSO site search facility.

The Statute Law Database

The Statutory Publication Office, an office within the Lord Chancellor's Department, is responsible for maintaining a database of primary and secondary legislation and is producing a database of United Kingdom legislation – the Statute Law Database (SLD) – which contains legislation dating from the Magna Carta to the present day and also prospective legislation.

This database will be completed in the year 2000 when it is planned to provide users (generally law publishers) with access to it via the internet, and to sell electronic copies of the data for purchasers to merge with their own products. The marketing and pricing strategy has not yet been finalised.

The database under development currently contains the text of all Acts that were current on 1 February 1991, together with most of the Acts and Statutory Instruments passed since then. It also contains local legislation, both primary and secondary. Currently, the main task of the Statutory Publications Office is to apply the effects of amending legislation on primary legislation. At present there are no plans to amend secondary legislation but this could be done if it was shown to be cost-effective.

The key feature of the central database being maintained by the Statutory Publications Office is that it will provide a historical view of primary legislation for any specific day from the base date of 1 February 1991 and any prospective legislation. Although secondary legislation is not being updated the enquiry system will facilitate the identification of any legislation that amends or repeals it.

The SLD is being developed by **Syntegra**, a BT company, and a demonstration version is available on the Syntegra Track Record website at www.syntegratrackrecord.co.uk. The demonstration version contains legislation for the years 1985 to 1995.

Parliamentary proceedings

www.parliament.uk

◆ **Hansard (House of Commons Debates)**

  · **Daily Debates including oral and written questions**
  · **Standing Committee Debates on Bills**
  · **Other Standing Committee Debates**

◆ **Public Bills before Parliament**

◆ **Private Bill Committee Reports**

◆ **Select Committee publications**

◆ **Other House of Commons Papers**

◆ **House Business ("*Vote Bundle*")**

  · **Summary Agenda and Order of Business**
  · **Future Business**
  · **Votes and Proceedings**
  · **European Community Documents**
  · **Public Bill List**
  · **Deregulation Proposals and Draft Orders**
  · **List of Statutory Instruments**
  · **Early Day Motions**
  · **Questions for Oral or Written Answer (The Order Book)**

◆ **Weekly Information Bulletin**

The **UK Parliament** site publishes both Commons' and Lords' Hansards, as well as Bills before Parliament, the Weekly Information Bulletin, Select Committee reports and Lords' judgments since November 1996.

The Bills listing gives the titles of public bills currently before Parliament which are available in full text on the site. At the head of each bill is a note of the stage which the bill has reached in its passage through Parliament. A complete list of public bills introduced in Parliament in the current session, together with information about their progress through Parliament, can be found in the Weekly Information Bulletin. Bills which have been passed by both Houses and have received Royal Assent as Acts of Parliament are available in full text on the HMSO legislation pages.

You can search the parliamentary databases, first selecting from a range of documents (Bills, Commons Hansards etc or All). Searches are either in your own words (free text) or by the name of an individual (speaker). You can also specifically include a Parliamentary Question number in your search, and optionally specify a date range.

There are equivalent resources on the **Scottish Parliament** site on the Parliamentary Business pages – see further Chapter 11 – and on the **Welsh Assembly** and the **Northern Ireland Assembly** sites. As the nomenclature is somewhat different in each jurisdiction and each site uses a distinctive design and layout, it is difficult to draw comparisons with the UK Parliament site. It is hoped that in the next edition guest authors from Wales and Northern Ireland will help us out!

Cases

Links to courts and cases are at www.infolaw.co.uk/ifl/law.htm#Courts and cases

House of Lords judgments

The texts of all **House of Lords** judgments delivered since 14 November 1996 are on the House of Lords pages on the Parliament site. New judgments appear online within two hours of delivery at the House.

Judgments are listed in alphabetical order. Presentation is unremarkable, with no external links. Texts are served up in 20 to 30K chunks, which reduces the initial download time but is frustrating if you want to scroll or search beyond the boundaries of the page.

To search the texts, use the Parliament search facility's drop down list and select Opinions of the Lords of Appeal.

The Court Service

COURT SERVICE

View Judgments
By Date

Court Service Web site
Companies Court

Previous Page | Next Page | Expand Headings | Collapse Headings

Title

Home
Search
View Selector
By Case Reference
By Date
By Defendant
By Judge
By Plaintiff
Index

▶ 31st July 1998
▼ 14th July 1998
▼ 14 July 1998 (Insolvency Act)
  ▶ Market Wizard Systems (UK) and The Insolvency Act 1986

Previous Page | Next Page | Expand Headings | Collapse Headings

Home | Search | By Case Reference | By Date | By Defendant | By Judge | By Plaintiff | Index

Selected judgments of the Court of Appeal and other divisions of the High Court started appearing on the **Court Service** site in Spring 1997. This presents a 'map' of the court structure and provides links to judgments, practice directions and daily lists for each of the courts, including the lower courts.

The number of judgments appearing on the site has increased greatly, though coverage is somewhat uneven as between the different courts. For many of the courts the judgments have been transferred to a searchable Domino database. Available judgments can be listed by case reference, by date or by the name of plaintiff, defendant or judge. You can also search the database using natural language terms, listing the results by relevance or in date order. Unfortunately the titles of many pages are not sufficiently specific, so the resulting listing is unhelpful. Most judgments are also aviailable for download as zipped Word documents.

Other law reports

General series:

Casebase from **Smith Bernal** is a free Court of Appeal transcript archive containing over 20,000 judgments from the Court of Appeal and Crown Office. No registration is required. The free service is currently limited to judgments in the previous calendar year. Additional services are available through the chargeable Casetrack subscription service – see further p 86.

Butterworths' All England Direct is the online version of the *All England Law Reports* – see further p 78.

The legal information services from **Lawtel**, **New Law Online** and **Sweet & Maxwell'**s Current Legal Information provide wide ranging case summaries on a chargeable basis. Full transcripts can also be ordered and delivered by mail, fax or email. These services are described in more detail in Chapter 4.

The **Incorporated Council of Law Reporting**'s Daily Law Notes provides free headnotes of selected High Court judgments.

The *Times Law Reports* are offered on **The Times** site, although only the current reports are available on the site (ie there is no archive available).

The **Law Society's Gazette** provides its extensive law reports, including property law reports, but, again, only current reports are available on the site.

Swarbrick & Co provide an index of over 9,000 case reports from January 1992 to date which can be searched by area of law as well as by date and by court.

Specialist reports:

Masons' Case Reports collects leading cases relating to the computer and telecommunications industries in a readily accessible form and provides authoritative commentary on each.

The **Estates Gazette Property Law Service** is a chargeable subscription service which includes Next Day reporting direct from the courts on cases of interest to the property industry, as well as the *Estates Gazette* Law Reports, Planning Law Reports and Lands Tribunal Decisions.

Gray's Inn Chambers provides a Tax Case Reporting Service – the intention is to put reports of significant tax cases online within 30 minutes.

Jordans' Family Law site provides summaries of recent family law decisions.

The **Employment Appeal Tribunal** provides its judgments in full text.

Court Practice and Procedures

Links to these sites are at www.infolaw.co.uk/ifl/law.htm#Civil procedure

The Court Service

The **Court Service** pages (see also p 26) provide an increasingly useful resource. For the Courts of Appeal and High Court there are links from each branch to Judgments (see p 55), Daily Lists, Notices and Practice Directions for that court.

The County Court section lists all courts and addresses and provides an index to determine which county court has geographical jurisdiction for a particular parish within England and Wales.

There are also links to Tribunal sites, including the Office of the Social Security and Child Support Commissioners, the Immigration Appellate Authority and the Special Commissioners of Income Tax.

The Forms and Leaflets pages include well indexed sets of many court forms, including the new civil procedure forms, in Adobe pdf format (see p 59).

Other texts published on the Court Service site include the Chancery Guide, the Commercial Court Guide, the Patents Court Guide, the Mercantile Court Guide and Fees Guidance.

The Civil Procedure Rules

THE LORD CHANCELLOR'S DEPARTMENT Civil Procedure Rules and Practice Directions Index	
PART 6 SERVICE OF DOCUMENTS	
See also **Practice Directions**	
CONTENTS OF THIS PART	
I GENERAL RULES ABOUT SERVICE	
Part 6 rules about service apply generally	Rule 6.1
Methods of service - general	Rule 6.2
Who is to serve	Rule 6.3
Personal service	Rule 6.4
Address for service	Rule 6.5

The official version of the new Civil Procedure Rules is on the **Lord Chancellor's Department** site on the Civil Matters page. This includes the Lord Chancellor's foreword, the Civil Procedure Rules, the Practice Directions, a

Glossary, the Schedules (ie surviving parts of the RSC/CCR) and the Pre-action Protocols. Amendments and further Practice Directions and Protocols are posted regularly.

The only means of navigation and access is back and forth from the main contents lists. Much of the information may be accessed in a number of different formats: as html (ie web) pages, as pdf documents or as Word documents.

The forms and explanatory leaflets are available from the **Court Service** site in pdf format.

The importance of the new Rules and their publication on the internet in this way has spawned a large number of alternative versions of the Rules and useful commentary sites.

Further information, updates and links to Civil Procedure sites are at www.infolaw.co.uk/ifl/cpr.htm.

Forms

Links to forms sites are at www.infolaw.co.uk/ifl/forms.htm

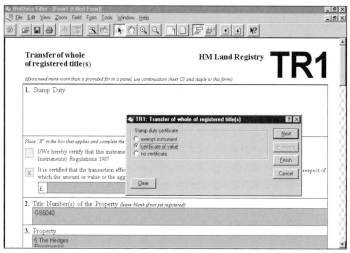

The HotDocs form filler in use

Many Government departments and agencies now publish versions of their forms on the web. These sites are of varying comprehensiveness and usefulness and are directed more towards the lay rather than the professional user. However, they are likely to become an increasingly useful resource with the move towards 'direct government'. (As to the future of form-filling in the information age, see p 63).

Forms on these sites are generally published in pdf format. pdf is Adobe Corporation's portable document format, effectively a viewable version of Adobe's PostScript print file format. pdf forms require that you have the Adobe Acrobat reader installed on your computer. This is available for free download from the **Adobe Corporation** site. When you access a pdf form on the web, you can either launch Acrobat to view the form or save it to disk for later viewing. pdf forms may be presented simply as images, in which case you can print copies but must fill them in by hand; or they may be fillable, in which case you can print the filled version. Whether or not you can save the filled form depends on the settings of the particular form and the version of Acrobat you are using.

Another popular format for forms publishing is HotDocs. To use HotDocs forms you need the HotDocs Player, available for free download from the **HotDocs** site. HotDocs forms are generally presented with intelligent question and answer dialogues. HotDocs fills the form and does any necessary calculations and computations and all data can be saved for later use. Forms may also be presented as tab-through, 'direct fill' forms. Forms are accessed either as a Hot-Docs library (hdi) for download or, since version 5, as auto-assemble files (hda) which effectively enable you to fill in the form on the web, saving the filled form and answer data (for reuse) locally.

Since Microsoft Word is so ubiquitous, forms may also be published as Word documents (protected Word forms) with or without some form of proprietary form filling interface.

Official forms sites

In its White Paper, *The Future Management of Crown Copyright* (see p 63), the Government recognises that is in its interest to make forms, both statutory and non-statutory, available as widely as possible and states that:

> It is therefore our intention to feature an increasing range of government forms on departmental websites in many cases enabling users to complete forms on screen.

The **Court Service** site is the first example of a substantial set of law forms available in this way. On the Forms and Leaflets pages is a wide range of the new Civil Procedure forms and the amended County Court forms, presented in pdf format. These are well organised into categories: Summons Forms, Forms before Judgment etc. Many of the forms are interactive and may be completed on screen with additional pop-up notes to assist in their completion.

Other departments are mostly well on their way to achieving similar levels of service.

The **Inland Revenue** publishes Self Assessment tax returns and help sheets in pdf format.

HM Customs & Excise publishes an extensive collection of customs, excise and VAT forms in pdf format.

On the **Patent Office** site there is a wide range of patent, trade mark, design and design and design right forms in pdf format.

The **Insolvency Service** publishes a handful of forms in pdf format.

The **Land Registry** publishes the 109 and 313forms in pdf format as well as a full 'emergency pack' of the latest batch (1999) of its new-style forms. For some strange reason the emergency pack of 1998 forms has been removed.

Although there is no official presence for the new **Legal Aid Board** forms, the full set of forms are available free of charge from the **Law Society** in HotDocs format.

Forms publishers' sites

The established names in forms publishing all now have websites, though the services actually available on the web vary widely.

Laserform Law provides access to form downloads for registered users only. There is currently no further information on the website.

Compuforms provides information and downloads for its forms which are in Word or WordPerfect Informs format. A forms-on-demand service enables you to fill in and print a form, using an on-screen web form interface, provided you have all the necessary software installed.

Proforma provides information on its range of automated HotDocs forms, more than 20 free forms for download, and forms update information, including a free newsletter, the *Proforma Informer*.

FormulaForms publishes downloadable Word forms and a free newsletter on registration.

Peapod provides detailed information on its range of forms.

Oyez Straker and **Shaw & Sons** provide summary information only.

Other forms and precedents

Many of the principal law publishers incorporate official forms and other forms and precedents in their products, and some of these are accessible through the web services they offer – see Chapter 4.

The **Precedent Exchange** is a forum for the exchange of precedents between lawyers. It offers access to a range of authored boilerplate templates and other precedents on the basis that users contribute a precedent of their own in exchange. It also provides an index to official forms sites.

Estates Gazette Interactive (EGi) provides Property Forms and Precedents derived from the Landlord and Tenant Acts, Assured Tenancies and Agricultural Occupancies (Forms) Regulations and other property-related sources. The forms are available in pdf format and can be downloaded from their site, filled in offline and then printed out.

Capsoft UK publish a selection of free HotDocs forms and precedents from HotDocs publishers, including Sweet & Maxwell, Croner Publications and Proforma.

Other Official Documents and Information

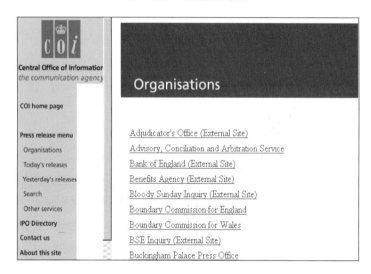

All official press releases can be accessed on the **Central Office of Information** site at www.coi.gov.uk/coi/. At the time of writing there is a hugely irritating changing graphic on the opening page – may it soon be removed. You can select from a list by Organisation, Today's Press Releases, Yesterday's Press Releases or Search the site.

The Stationery Office maintains an Official Documents site at www.official-documents.co.uk. The site provides selected UK Command Papers, including White Papers and Green Papers and other consultative documents as well as links to all other official document sites (HMSO, Parliament etc). Documents can be listed by date, by title or by department.

Confusingly The Stationery Office's official online presence, TSOnline, at www.tsonline.co.uk is more of a shop front for its hardcopy publishing and does not appear anywhere to point to the Official Documents site.

The **CCTA Government Information Service** (see also p 12) provides links to many government departments and organisations, including regulatory bodies. There is a search engine relating to all UK government servers (including local government) and a What's New section containing government press releases.

Information Age Government

In early 1999, the Government published two papers of great import:

- The White Paper, *The Future Management of Crown Copyright*, lays the foundations for a flexible and responsive management system, and establishes the Government Information Asset Register.

- The document *Modernising Government* (on the Official Documents site at www.official-documents.co.uk/document/cm43/4310/4310.htm) sets out the Government's aims in delivering direct government to businesses and citizens in the information age.

Crown copyright

Many respondents [to the Green Paper, *Crown Copyright in the Information Age*] recognised the need to preserve the integrity and official status of government material. It was generally perceived that Crown copyright operates as a brand or kitemark of quality indicating the status and authority of much of the material produced by Government. However, Crown copyright can be asserted and then waived to ensure light touch management, particularly for material of a legislative or consultative nature, where it is in Government's interests to encourage unrestricted use.

Consequently, formal and specific licensing will not be necessary for the following categories of material (inter alia):

- Primary and secondary legislation
- Explanatory notes to legislation
- Government press notices
- Government forms
- Government consultative documents
- Government documents featured on official departmental websites

This permission extends the former concession made by HMSO under which publishers were permitted to reproduce the above categories of information only in a 'value-added context'.

A distinction is drawn between Crown copyright materials produced to meet core obligations or statutory duties, which are freely copiable, and services where value has been added by Government, when such information is potentially tradable and copying is not permitted. For example, the putative Statute Law Database is a value-added service which will not be copiable, though the statutory texts themselves will be.

The Government recognises that it is in its interest to make forms, both statutory and non-statutory, available as widely as possible and states that 'It is therefore our intention to feature an increasing range of government forms on departmental websites in many cases enabling users to complete forms on screen.' The first example of a substantial set of law forms available inthis way is the new civil procedure forms on the Court Service site. See further Forms, p 59.

The new regime will ensure a much wider and more rapid distribution of statutory and related texts than hitherto, encouraging smaller publishers (and on the web, we are all publishers) to adapt these materials to their own use.

The Information Asset Register

The Government accepts the principle that departments should produce regularly updated listings of material which they hold. ... Our aim is to provide a gateway and central information point to guide and direct a route through the maze of official government information and materials ... which we call the Government Information Asset Register (IAR).

The IAR will provide an effective retrieval tool to complement the existing routes via departmental and other cross-government websites providing broad categories of information with links through to these other sites.

The Information Asset Register's records will include the following information: Title, Identifier/Database Acronym, Description, Source Language, Creator, Format(s), Date made available, Updating frequency, Subject keywords, Geographic coverage, Contact/Distributor and Rights.

Work on development of the IAR started at the end of 1998. It currently contains some sample entries and links to the existing bibliographic databases. Information Asset Registers will be added as these come on stream with the aim that most departmental entries will complete during the year 2000.

Information age government

We will use new technology to meet the needs of citizens and business, and not trail behind technological developments.

The Government is taking specific actions to develop information age government through IT in a number of areas. In many cases this is allowing public services to be delivered 24 hours a day, seven days a week and the Government promises to continue to promote initiatives to modernise services in accordance with the needs of citizens and businesses.

For example, from 2000, individual taxpayers and businesses will be able to make income tax returns to the Inland Revenue and register for VAT with Customs & Excise over the Internet. In the Budget, the Government announced that there would be a discount for small businesses which make their tax returns electronically.

By 2002, the Government intends, as a minimum, that business will be able electronically to:

- complete VAT registration and make VAT returns.
- file returns at Companies House.
- apply for regional support grants.
- receive payments from government for the supply of goods and services.

To bring about a more coherent approach to the use of websites for giving information and eventually delivering services, it will publish guidelines for government websites by November 1999 and relaunch the site www.open.gov.uk. so that it provides easier access to information and an updated search facility.

In the longer term, the Government aims to link the widest possible range of government services and information through electronic government gateways (or portals).

The Prime Minister announced in 1997 that, by 2002, 25% of dealings with Government should be capable of being done by the public electronically. Progress towards this target (the '25% Initiative) is published on a six-monthly basis by the **Central IT Unit** (CITU) of the Cabinet Office at www.citu.gov.uk and the Government proposes that 50% of dealings should be capable of electronic delivery by 2005 and 100% by 2008.

Online Journals and Legal Newspapers

Links to legal journals, and also more general newspapers, are at
www.venables.co.uk/legal/news.htm

The Lawyer

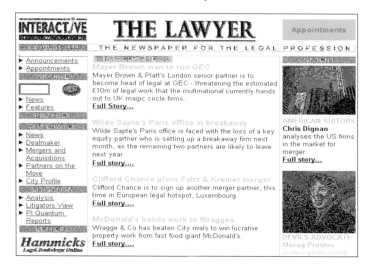

The Lawyer has now an extensive and useful online presence with most of the printed paper available (free) online.

In some respects, the paper online is better than in print, since you can access past issues as well as the current one. The archive goes back to 1994 and all articles, features, letters, profiles and stories over this period can be accessed using a searching mechanism.

The current edition can be accessed in various ways, as can be seen in the left hand frame of the picture above, for example, you can select all the stories concerning partners on the move for quick viewing.

An advantage of the online presentation, from the paper's point of view, is that it can provide cross-advertising to other parts of the Centaur Group (to Lawtel, or to various Lawyer-sponsored conferences) or to advertisers' websites, presumably for a fee. There is a particular feature of linking to recruitment consultants' websites, or special sections on the job page set aside for individual recruitment consultants (covered later in this chapter).

The Law Society's Gazette

There is a great deal of useful material available on the **Law Society's Gazette** website – indeed most of the printed journal is available online. However, detailed stories and features are not shown in any sort of a list, to enable the viewer to select the ones of interest. In fact, the text is obviously stored in blocks, looking rather like the printed page, but without any internal links or ways to move around (apart from scrolling around, with the mouse). Thus, for example, if you select the general news option, you have to scroll through the whole set of pages relating to this, with no way of moving quickly to something which interests you.

The In Practice section, which includes the Law Reports, is a useful resource. Another useful feature is the Gazette Daily which allows stories to be presented in between the printed versions.

The recruitment sections work well, which are described in a later section.

The Gazette seems to have made over the top quarter of the available screen to advertising. This does seem to be a pity.

In Brief

In Brief has an attractive site with a lot of potential, although much of the material is not, at the time of writing, yet present.

There are only a few stories provided on the site each month. In addition, the Technology for Lawyers consists only of information about the 'Loties' awards and the Appointments Section is not yet in operation. The Restaurant Section is also 'In construction'.

The Bluffers Guide is present – it consists of a series of stories about major firms, taken from past issues.

The World Legal Forum may well build up into an interesting resource, bringing in stories on each country from past issues of the journal, and news relating to these firms, but it is as yet only just starting. In due course it will provide direct links to these firms.

Computers & Law

The **Society for Computers and Law**'s journal is one of the main sources of current and well researched articles on the law relating to information technology as well as IT for lawyers.

The journal is presented fully online and, on occasions, articles appear on the site before the printed journal appears. Although the SCL has left open the option of allowing access only to members (there is a password required to use part of the site), this has never in fact been fully implemented and all viewers are cordially informed that the password is 'sclonline'. Long may it last.

Journal of Information, Law and Technology

The **Journal of Information, Law and Technology** (JILT) from the Universities of Warwick and Strathclyde is another useful journal with well researched papers (it comes out three times a year). Sometimes the articles are just 'flat' printed text but on other occasions the medium is fully utilised with extensive links and sections included from many sources.

One memorable past article (30 June 1997) covered the AustLII developments (the full text and multiply interlinked legal resource set up in Australia). Called 'The AustLII Papers – New Directions in Law via the Internet' by Prof Graham Greenleaf et al, the article covered not only the AustLII site as it is now but also the implications for law reporting in the future. This was an article which would not have been nearly so interesting or informative in a printed book.

Legal Technology Insider

The **Legal Technology Insider** is an excellent fortnightly newsletter on developments in legal IT, compiled and edited by Charles Christian. The newsletter itself is not online for free but subscribers can access an html version, either for individual use or for use on an intranet. The advantage of this method of distribution is that many people can then view the newsletter from their desks.

The html version is fully equipped with hyperlinks to the companies, firms or sites mentioned, which is a useful way of presenting the information.

Internet Newsletter for Lawyers

The *Internet Newsletter for Lawyers*, published in hardcopy and html versions by Delia Venables, aims to cover all the stories of interest to lawyers concerning internet topics:

- New free current awareness resources
- What the publishers are offering
- Legal developments concerning the internet and e-commerce
- Practical aspects of setting up a website, finding a suitable web services company or doing it yourself, getting the site registered in the search engines, and then keeping it up to date
- Examples of interesting sites set up by solicitors and barristers themselves
- Examples of firms gaining work over the web
- Practical aspects of handling email in an organisation.

The Newsletter is not itself on Delia Venables' website for free, but the html version can be loaded onto a firm's intranet.

Newsletters by Email

Links to the newsletter sites described are at www.venables.co.uk/legal/aware.htm

As well as offering information on the web, many sites also offer online newsletters by email. Subscribers (no money is involved) simply fill in a form on screen with their details and send it to the publisher and thereafter they receive a regular (or irregular) email with useful information.

From the publisher's point of view, this is a means of proving expertise very cheaply – the costs of distributing a newsletter by email are effectively nil.

Here are some of the email newsletters currently on offer:

Bretherton Price & Elgoods offers a series of free email Legal Alerts in employment, company/commercial, corporate finance, commercial property and commercial litigation. You can register on the site and select which areas of law you wish to receive information about.

CMS Cameron McKenna offers a service called LawNow which provides an email information service on any of a large number of topics, which can be selected by the viewer.

Fox Williams offers Newsletters by email on IT and Cyberlaw. You can register on the site.

E-Business + Law, edited by **Charles Christian**, and sponsored by Jeffrey Green Russell and Solicitec, comes out once a month with news, comment and analysis. To register, email Charles Christian. There is an archive of back issues on the site.

Nabarro Nathanson offers an email update based on their latest Legal briefings and news items. You can register on the site. Take the Legal Briefings option.

Paisner & Co offer a free online alerting service called eBRIEF which will provide information on current computer, media and intellectual property (CMIP) issues and on regulatory law issues such as licensing, food law and health and safety.

As well as the E-Business + Law newsletter described on an earlier page, Charles Christian prepares and distributes two further email newsletters:

- Local Government Law Watching Brief
- Litigation Support Digital Newsletter.

You can see details of the newsletters (and back numbers) and register for the newsletters on the **Legal Technology Insider** site.

Legal Software and Information Technology Suppliers

For links to lawtech suppliers see www.venables.co.uk/legal/software.htm and www.infolaw.co.uk/ifl/supplier.htm

The majority of the 60 companies who supply legal software and who have a website are still providing brochure sites.

Many of these sites are attractive and informative, if a little unexciting.

Of the websites which are doing more than providing some basic online literature about their products, the material seems to fall into three categories:

- Providing free software or forms as a taster promotion.
- Providing evaluation versions of the software and/or selling software or forms directly over the web.
- Providing support over the web.

Free software or forms

Generally speaking suppliers are not in the business of giving away their software for free, but forms are in a rather different category – once the user has learnt the basic techniques of downloading and using a particular type of form, he or she may well become a serious customer for further forms. For details of the wide range of forms available on the web, both free and chargeable, see p 59.

Another example of the type of free legal software available is the Expense of Time Calculator from **MSS**, based on the Law Society's booklet (fifth edition).

Evaluation copies of software and direct sales

Most legal software is too large and complex for easy trials or downloads of this sort. An evaluation without support or training could put the potential user right off the product, rather than giving a good impression.

However, a few companies do offer trial versions of their software, including:

- the document and case management system **Amicus Attorney** (picture overleaf);
- the Advocate (a program for criminal lawyers) for the Psion computer from Julian Gibbons of **Crimefile**; and
- Legacy UK Will Writer from **HSC**.

Providing support over the web

It would be a major advantage to the suppliers of legal software if they could persuade their users to accept support services over the web. If even a proportion of

the queries which normally go through to the support desk could be answered in this way, without direct human contact, real savings to the suppliers (and ultimately to the users) could be made. However, this is only just beginning. One supplier said that a user had become quite uppity when such a suggestion was made; he was paying for telephone support and did not want to be fobbed off by web support!

The irony here is that the suppliers themselves are now receiving – whether they like it or not – a great deal of their support over the web. As Steve Ness of **Select Systems** says:

> The suppliers with whom we have support contracts (SCO, Informix, DELL etc) now provide all of their first line support information over the web and it works very well. Their support information is professionally collated, indexed and presented and as a result it is very easy to find an answer to most problems. Legal suppliers such as ourselves will need to provide the same quality of support information. Technically there is no problem and I think both parties can ultimately benefit a great deal. I believe the only problem is an educational (and maybe a financial) one. Most if not all of the employees at a legal firm must progress to the point where they use the web as an everyday tool of the trade and that is when we can be confident that using the web is going to be effective. I think this could still take 3–5 years.

Some suppliers are already offering users the option of receiving software updates and user support over the web, including Axxia, Capsoft, Lexology, MSS, Pilgrim, Solicitec and Videss.

Solicitec is using its own web-enabled software called SolCase Online, to accept queries and problems from their users and then track through to the solutions.

This is an interesting use of the software which they sell to solicitors to enable the solicitors to provide web access to their systems. Once the problem is logged, the user can access Solicitec's site at any time to follow progress.

Videss offer a special area for user support, controlled by password (only registered Videss users can access this part of the site).

The FAQ's (Frequently Asked Questions) provide a series of answers to questions which have arisen in the past.

The instruction manuals offers a full download of a complete manual (a fairly lengthy procedure) whilst the Quick Reference Fact Sheets offers quick summaries of these manuals. The Support Bulletin and Version Information together cover support schedules and the facilities available in various program updates whilst the newsletter provides more general information about new developments generally.

The section Who are Videss Support Desk is a nice touch – it provides pictures and short biographies of the people on the support desk (the online support is not intended to replace the telephone support but to supplement it).

The discussion forum is a good idea but does not yet seem to be used – perhaps this is an indication of the fact that the web-based support facilities are not yet used by a high proportion of the users.

Expert Witnesses

For links to expert witness sites, see www.venables.co.uk/legal/experts.htm

There are many individual expert witnesses with their own websites but it is impossible to know, from the individual websites, whether the person concerned is in fact qualified or suitable for the job. Here, we cover some of the main registers and organisations set up by and for expert witnesses which do (it must be hoped) provide some level of authentication of the experts concerned.

The **Academy of Experts** provides a register of Experts and Qualified Dispute Resolvers. This can be searched by discipline and by geographic area.

ExpertSearch (UK) provides a large register of UK expert witnesses, containing over 3,300 profiles, an online database (searchable by name, town, county, region, qualification or area of expertise) an unusual 'email directory' containing the email addresses of over 1,000 UK expert witnesses and over 400 links to UK expert witnesses' own websites.

The **Great Britain Internet Register of Expert Witnesses** is another substantial list of experts with search facilities and full details.

The **UK Register of Expert Witnesses** from JS Publications is apparently the longest established independent listing of vetted expert witnesses and the full register of 3,000 experts is now online. As for most of these organisations, you have to register to use the searching facility but it is free. There are apparently 17,000 terms which can be selected to aid in a detailed search. The site also provides a great deal of information about expert witnesses in general – how to use them and how to be one.

There are also quite a number of organisations based in the USA of which we give here just a few. Some of these are now including international experts.

The **Expert Witness Network**, previously Legal Research Network (LERN), links attorneys and expert witnesses 'to reduce the time and costs associated with locating the best expert for a case'.

Expert Law is a register of expert witnesses, designed for use by lawyers and also by members of the public. International experts (including from the UK) can register, free of charge.

Law Info can be used to locate attorneys, expert witnesses, and other legal information of use to members of the public.

Expert Pages describes itself as the original and leading Internet directory of expert witnesses and consultants.

Jobs Online

The online jobs market seems to be divided into two sections:

- the legal journals, who have traditionally carried job vacancies, and who display full details of the jobs, with a reference number for applying for the job; and

- agencies and recruitment consultants, who give away as little as possible online and whose real aim is to gather CVs and provide full information only to the people on its books.

For the casual viewer, only the former category is of real interest, and we will cover these first.

The Lawyer, in its online version, carries all the advertisements of the printed journal.

This is a search on Property – all regions. Each of the underlined heading leads to a full section on the job concerned. There are typically around 450 jobs available at any time and these can be searched by region, sector, speciality and level of PQE or browsed all at once.

The Lawyer also provides a lists of appointment consultants with details about each, which can be of use if deciding which to choose. If the recruitment consultants have a website of their own, the link is given, but most do not yet have one. You can also see cross sections of the jobs relating to particular appointment consultants.

The **Law Society's Gazette** provides all its advertisements online and you can search by region or specialism and by the particular consultant providing the service.

In Brief, the monthly magazine, has a section for jobs on its website, but at the time of writing (August 1999) the jobs are not there yet.

Moving now to the Recruitment Consultants, there are perhaps a dozen of the main companies online so far.

Garfield Robbins only gives the viewer about two lines of information on each job – not enough to decide whether you really like the sound of it. Basically, they want you to submit your CV and register with them.

QD Group is another recruitment consultant company offering you tasters only and wanting you to register with them. However, there is a little more information available than in the Garfield Robbins site.

One Hundred Percent Recruitment is a new recruitment agency which provides legal staffing for law firms and law departments in corporate firms.

Jobs for Lawyers UK is another new company offering jobs which can be searched on the site. There is also a section (not yet large) on trainee and pupil opportunities. This company does not require you to register your cv – you can just browse.

gti – UK & Irish Graduate careers – cover many career areas (not just the law). The site is a bit trendy with themes covering the sections of the site, eg footballers. The connections to the jobs offered are not terribly obvious.

PSD is an international recruitment organisation with various areas of specialisation including the law.

Zarak Macrae Brenner (ZMB) is another international agency with various areas of specialisation including the law. Apparently, it has 300 jobs on its books. You can browse to a certain extent, once you have entered your search criteria.

Other Recuitment Consultants on line include HW Group, ERS Legal, Career Legal Professional and Michael Page.

Chapter 4

Law Publishers on the Web

Contents

This chapter describes the extensive material for legal research now provided by the legal publishers on the internet. The descriptions are based on information provided by the publishers themselves. If any point is of particular importance to you, please check it with the publisher concerned. Almost all of the publishers offer a free trial of their services; this is a wonderful opportunity to find out what is available and decide which service is best adapted to your needs.

No attempt is made to indicate or compare the costs of these services. Costs vary for the type of organisation concerned and the level of use required. The costs are also changing all the time as the publishers struggle with the complicated licencing agreements which are necessary for internet use. Decide, first of all, which service you actually want, taking advantage of the free trials on offer, and only then discuss with the publisher the cost of the service. Competition is fierce and all the publishers are very keen to get new subscribers.

The terms 'web' or 'internet-based' refer to services offered directly on the internet, accessed via your normal service provider and using your normal web browser (Netscape or Internet Explorer). The term 'online' is often used to mean a service where you dial in direct to the information provider. Reference is also made to information on CD-ROM, which is very suitable for research where large amounts of information are needed for access and where it is not essential to have access to the very latest developments. Some services now offer a CD with online (or web) updating facility for the latest information.

General Law Publishers and Law Reporting Services

Butterworths

www.butterworths.co.uk

Free services

News Direct, an online legal newspaper, with current stories, features, a diary page, appointments, Moneyfacts, video clips and a calendar of events. There are also Irish and Scottish versions available.

Woolf tracking service: containing an Updater to the Civil Court Practice which links to the full updated text of the Civil Court Rules and Practice Directions. The service also contains a bimonthly newsletter, the Civil Court News, which provides updates and analysis of the latest developments in civil procedure including recent case law, practice directions and amending statutory instruments.

Year 2000 information and links covering legal, technical and commercial issues of Y2K.

Academic site, with chapters from the 'Student Law in Context' series, online ordering, case notes and a tour of UK universities.

Updates to selected books, legal links, and an online version of the *New Law Journal*.

Subscription services

Crime Online (provided with Blackstone Press), which includes a daily updating service delivering new cases, SIs, legislation and announcements; an archive of SIs, Statutes and Practice Directions, plus access to 3,000 criminal cases in the *All England Law Reports* and thousands of official manuscripts; and the full text of Blackstone's *Criminal Practice* and other important narrative information.

Halsbury's Laws Direct, an online version of *Halsbury's Laws of England*, regularly updated. A facility called Eureka enables the user to find information using 'plain English'. Direct links are provided to Butterworths' other online services.

All England Direct, with online access to the *All England Law Reports*, 1936 to date. In addition, there is an archive of official transcripts, with detailed subject categorisation and updated parallel cites. There is also a current awareness service with next day delivery of digests of cases with corresponding judgments delivered on approval by the judge.

Tax Direct, with news and full text of tax developments, including an email alerter service and the latest editions of *Taxation* and *Tax Journal*. There is also an archive of articles from *Tax Journal*, *Taxation*, Tolley's *Practical Tax*, VAT Service and NIC Service. The News Service includes a comprehensive tax case reporting service and tax offices addresses. The subscriber has a choice of buying the Tax Direct News Service module and/or the Tax Direct Reference Service which includes at least 13 of the most famous tax reference manuals, from the Simon's range of products to Butterworths Yellow and Orange Handbooks.

PI Direct, with Quantum cases database, Civil Procedure Rules, the Butterworths Personal Injury Litigation Service, cases from the *All England Law Reports*, expert witness database, a calculation facility for damages and a weekly journal.

Local Government Direct, with law updates, news update supplied in conjunction with LGCnet, legislation, cases, information from the *Local Government Reports*, practice manuals (Butterworths Local Government Law and Local Authority Companies and Partnerships), precedents and an 'online community'.

Legislation Direct, with the full (amended) text of all Acts and SI's of general application in England and Wales (around 17,000) cross-referenced to each other by hypertext.

Law Direct: a current awareness product with three main elements:

- Daily Update: a 24 hour legal alerter service presenting fully categorised summaries of Acts of Parliament, SI's, cases, European legislation and quasi-legal material, including Green and White papers, Law Commission papers, Government Press Releases and consultative documents.

- A Weekly Web Journal: providing contextual analysis of the latest legal developments by leading practitioners.

- Supplementary Databases:

Is it in Force? With commencement information on all statutes of general application published over the past twenty-five years.

Progress of Legislation database with daily information on the stage bills have reached and summaries of those bills and their intent.

Civil Procedure Service with the full updated text of the Civil Court Rules and Practice Directions, updated as soon as amendments are made.

Archive databases which include all cases, Acts and SIs since 1995.

EC Brief service, aimed at keeping the busy practitioner up-to-date with EU developments, updated daily, structured into practice areas and sub-categories. A full document delivery service is also available.

Also included are an articles citator, transcript ordering service, trademarks database (all UK and EU trademarks), expert witness database and a Company Search facility, in association with aRMadillo Online.

Contact 0845 608 1188 or karen.farman@butterworths.co.uk. A free 7-day trial is available.

CCH New Law Online

ww.cchnewlawonline.com and www.cchnewlaw.co.uk

Subscription services

CCH New Law (a division of Croner Publications Ltd) provides an online database of English and European judgments. These are selected by a team of qualified barristers, edited, digested and cross-referenced.

All areas of law are covered (except for Family and Immigration).

Courts covered: High Court, Court of Appeal, House of Lords, Privy Council, European Court of Justice, Employment Appeal Tribunal, Patent Office, Trade Marks Registry, Special Commissioners, VAT and Duties Tribunal and Pensions Ombudsman.

Services: Digests of judgments the day they are given, transcripts of judgments, extracted references and cross-referenced database.

Two types of services are offered: the Digest and the Online service.

The Digest Service comprises case summaries faxed or e-mailed on a daily basis. Transcripts of the digested cases can be ordered on payment of a small additional fee.

The Online Service is a database of cases comprising the same digests sent out to Digest subscribers and transcripts of those cases. These are cross-referenced and hyper-linked therefore enabling subscribers to carry out research.

Contact Alison Eyet on 020 7405 5434 or ale@croner.co.uk.

The CCH Employment Law Service is a specialist service. This provides:

Database of comprehensive commentary providing complete A–Z coverage of employment law linked to a dedicated current awareness service providing one source edited coverage of news and information, legislative developments, press releases, cases, news from Parliament and events.

Case database: summarises, digests, and selected full text judgements from the EAT, High Court, Court of Appeal, House of Lords and ECJ and Pensions Ombudsman's determinations. Overnight daily updating of the case database with digests from the appellate tribunal and courts.

Employment Lawyer, printed journal covering the EAT, High Court, Court of Appeal, House of Lords, ECJ and employment tribunal case digests with specialist comment.

Monthly employment law case reporting service providing a compilation of the month's leading cases with full-text judgements with headnotes and specialist comment.

Employment Law Reports – case book (bound), an annual compilation of all the leading employment law cases.

Contact 01869 872469 for a free trial.

Context

www.justis.com

Subscription services

Context provides legal and government information for the UK and Europe under the Justis brand. The information is available on CD-ROM, with an online service to provide the latest information, or directly on the Internet.

electronic Law Reports contains the full archive of the Law Reports from 1865 and is available on CD or on Justis.com. The reports are split into the following divisions: Appeal Cases, Queen's Bench, Chancery and Family.

Justis Weekly Law includes the full archive of volumes 1, 2 and 3 of the *Weekly Law Reports*, and is available on CD or on Justis.com.

The Law Reports Digest contains the full citation, catchwords, headnote and references of every case from the *Weekly Law Reports* and the *Law Reports*. Not published by the Incorporated Council of Law Reporting since 1950, this material is available exclusively on Justis.com.

Justis UK Statutes contains the full text of all Acts of Parliament since the Magna Carta of 1235, with links to all amending and amended legislation. Includes repealed Acts, and all Scottish Acts. It is currently available on CD only.

Justis UK Statutory Instruments contains the full text of SIs from 1987, including tables, diagrams and maps. Available on CD and on Justis.com.

Justis CELEX comprises the official database of the European Communities with the full text of treaties, legislation and proposed legislation from the European Court of Justice. Versions in English, French and German are available. CD and Justis.com.

Tenders on the Web (www.tenders.co.uk) is a database of public sector contracts from the UK, EU, USA and Japan. Updated five days a week it contains all documents published in the Supplement to the *Official Journal* of the European Communities with $400 Billion worth of business opportunities per year, including many lucrative contracts for legal services.

Contact Enquiries@context.co.uk or call 020 7267 8989.

W Green & Son

www.wgreen.co.uk

Free services

Latest news from the *Scots Law Times* with outline contents of case reports and news on legal matters and appointments in Scotland.

Articles and Scottish legal links, a forum for discussion on Scottish legal topics and a catalogue of publications with an online ordering service and sample chapters from new books.

Contact Jane Scott at Jane.Scott@wgreen.co.uk.

The Incorporated Council of Law Reporting for England and Wales

www.lawreports.co.uk

Free service

Daily Law Notes contains summarised reports of cases heard at House of Lords and Privy Council, Court of Appeal Criminal and Civil Divisions, Chancery Division, Queen's Bench Division, Family Division and Court of Justice of the European Communities.

The site contains case summaries written by the reporters (all barristers and solicitors) on the day that judgment is handed down. The summarised report of the case is available on the site within 24 hours. Not all cases are covered; the same principles are used as apply to the *Weekly Law Reports* and the *Law Reports*, ie that a case must introduce a new principle or a new rule, materially modify an existing principle or rule, settle a point upon which the law is doubtful or be peculiarly instructive for some reason.

The cases reported here have been summarised and are not the full text version that will appear in due course in the *Weekly Law Reports*, the *Law Reports* or the *Industrial Cases Reports*.

Cases are indexed under the court it was heard and will also alphabetically by subject matter (as in the Cumulative Index of cases the 'Red Book').

Other services on the site include details of recent, current and forthcoming law reports, a student newsletter and advertisements for second-hand sets of law reports for sale and wanted.

Contact postmaster@iclr.co.uk or 020 72426471.

Lawtel

www.lawtel.co.uk

Subscription services

Daily Update. Current awareness service delivering a bulletin of all legal developments every 24 hours and including Case Law, Legislation, Articles, Practice Directions and PI Quantum Reports. Daily Updates can be viewed online or received in a variety of email formats.

Full Daily Update. Covers all areas of the law. When accessed online, each entry in the bulletin is linked to the entire Lawtel document. The Full Daily Update is also available as an email or as an attached Word, Word Perfect, or Rich Text format file.

Customised Daily Updates. Daily Updates can be tailored according to speciality by selecting from a list of over 100 areas of the law or by database. These can be received online as a customised web page or delivered directly to your desktop as an email, now available in html format.

Period Updates can be generated for a specific time period.

Case Law. Cases from all areas of the law are available online within 24 hours of judgment. Sources include: House of Lords, Privy Council, Court of Appeal (Civil and Criminal Divisions); Queen's Bench Division including Divisional Court, Crown Office, Commercial Court, Admiralty Court; Chancery Division including Companies Court, Patents Court, Restrictive Practices Court, Bankruptcy Court, Revenue List; Family Division; Technology & Construction Court; other courts and tribunals including Employment Appeal Tribunal, Copyright Tribunal, Lands Tribunal, VAT and Duties Tribunal, Special Commissioners; Crown Court and County Court.

Coverage. Hundreds of unreported cases every month appear on Lawtel the day after judgment is given, often weeks ahead of any other source. If cases are subsequently reported elsewhere, Lawtel will add references from over 20 leading specialist and general law reports.

Fully searchable archive contains over 25,000 decisions and includes all the major law reports since 1980 plus thousands of decisions reported exclusively by Lawtel. Significant cases decided before 1980 have also been added as they are cited in later case law.

Transcripts Express. Document delivery service providing the full text of any official transcript, article or EU document.

Legislation. The following Lawtel legislative databases are available to track the legislative process: Statute Law, Commencements & Repeals, Statutory Instruments, Parliamentary Bills, Command Papers.

Articles Index. Abstracts of substantive, discursive, legal and practice management articles from over 50 major legal titles, including the legal sections of the major broadsheets. Search by subject, title, publication, author, date, case law or legislation (UK and European).

Case Citator including the European Court Of Justice (ECJ) and Court of First Instance (CFI) and Legislation Citator covering Statutes, Statutory Instruments, EU Law and Proposed Legislation are also available.

Interactive Lawyer is a series of special services for the specialist lawyer. Each Interactive Lawyer centre includes: *The Lawyer*, news and analysis, vacancies and Lawtel's Case Law, Legislation and Articles Index. Available so far (more to come):

Civil Procedure Interactive – Full text of the latest version of the Civil Procedure Rules, their Schedules, Personal Injury and Clinical Negligence Pre-Action Protocols, Practice Directions plus the Commercial Court Guide online. The latest cases and articles on the application of the rules are available the day after publication. Simmons & Simmons provide a running commentary on the provisions.

PI Interactive – Comprehensive online information service for personal injury lawyers providing access to 10 new services including: PI Weekly Update; PI Quantum Reports; PI Liability Reports; PI Articles Index; JSB Guidelines (4th Edition); and PI Actuarial Tables.

EU Interactive – A fully indexed database of over 90,000 EU documents dating back to 1987. All official EU documents are available online within 24 hours of release. Includes: Full coverage of all ECJ, CFI and Advocate-General Opinions. Adopted and Proposed Legislation including the Official Journals L and C series. EU Articles Index and Background Information covering Commission reports, Press Releases, Newsletters, European Parliament Questions and Notices are also available. The full text of any EU document dating back to 1953 can be ordered.

Local Government Interactive for lawyers in the public sector.

Contact Katy Adelson on 020 7970 4834 or katya@centaur.co.uk.

Lexis-Nexis

www.lexis-nexis.co.uk

Lexis was the first legal online service in the UK, operating until now with special access software and a special phone number. The service is now known as Lexis-Nexis and is also now available on the web using normal browser software.

Free services

Daily news on European Court of Human Rights, European Monetary Union and European Investment News.

Subscription services

There are four services available on the web, called respectively Professional, Executive, Alert Personal and Alert. The service which includes the legal material is the Professional Service. This offers everything previously available with the traditional Lexis, but now also available via the internet as part of the Lexis-Nexis service.

For added internet security, these four products are also available with web-browser access but not over the public internet, using the LNET Dialler – a CD-ROM which loads the web browser on the user's PC but connects to the Lexis-Nexis database via traditional dial-up access methods. This hybrid offers familiar web-browser searching but with a secure connection.

Reported Cases – the full text from over 30 sets of leading law reports since 1945, with the All England Reports from 1936 and Tax Cases from 1875 and many specialised series of reports, eg Construction law, Property law, Company Commercial law, and Intellectual Property.

Unreported Cases – transcripts of 43,000 unreported cases from the High Court and above dating back to 1980 with new transcripts available within days of official approval. All cases are fully searchable and are reference checked by a team of experienced legal editors.

Northern Ireland – general case law as reported in the *Northern Ireland Law Reports* from 1945 and unreported cases from 1984.

Scots Law – over 14,000 Scots cases including reported decisions from the *Scots Law Times* from 1945, Session cases from 1944, Criminal Case Reports from 1981 and Civil Case Reports from 1986.

The total archive of cases, reported and unreported, consists of over 114,000 English cases, 14,000 Scots Law cases and 3,000 cases from Northern Ireland.

Legislation – fully amended current legislation of England and Wales. This includes all Public General Acts still in force as well as any Statutory Instruments which are in force under the provisions of any Public General Acts (not local Statutory Instruments).

Current Awareness – based initially on Halsbury's Monthly Law Review, the library includes new developments in all the categories above as well as the progress of bills and a table of quantum of damages.

News and Business Service – news and business sources from around the world, including wide coverage of UK newspapers and periodicals.

Also: comprehensive collections of European, Commonwealth, International and USA materials.

Republic of Ireland – Irish case law including cases reported in Irish Reports, Irish Law Reports Monthly, Irish Law Times and Judgments of the Court of Criminal Appeal (Frewen). Selected unreported cases from 1985.

Contact 020 7464 1300 or response@lexis-nexis.com for a free trial.

Smith Bernal

www.smithbernal.com

Smith Bernal are the Official Reporters to the Courts of Appeal and developers of the award winning real-time transcription software, LiveNote.

Free service

Casebase is a free archive of Court of Appeal and Crown Office judgments from 1996 to 1998. Cases can be searched using case name, date, court and case number. New judgments are added on an annual basis.

Note also that the Casetrack service (see below), which is normally a subscription service, is available free to academic institutions, charities and welfare organisations.

Subscription service

Casetrack is a tracking, research and full text retrieval system for all Court of Appeal, High Court and EAT cases. Casetrack is the only comprehensive source of all new judgments from these courts.

The service provides internet access to all judgments from 1998 onwards. Case records contain key details about cases plus the full text of each judgment. The transcript can be read/printed on screen or detached and incorporated within a users own archive or know-how system.

Features include instant access to new judgments as soon as they have been approved. As the Official Reporters to the Courts of Appeal and Crown Office and the transcriber in the majority of ex tempore High Court cases, Smith Bernal are uniquely placed to ensure the fastest access to new judgments. The record is 26 minutes for attachment of a handed down approved case. All handed down approved judgments from the Court of Appeal and Crown Office are available within 24 hours of judgment being given.

Searching by core fields, subject search and full text capabilities. All judgments are indexed according to a range of search parameters ensuring that users can find cases regardless of how much information they have. Full text searching allows research using key facts, principles or precedent (case or statute).

Tracking – status of judgments from listing to approval. Skeleton cases are created as soon as a case is listed for judgment. New details are added to the case record based on each day's activity in the courts allowing you to see whether the judgment has been given, reserved or part heard and whether the judgment is available or in draft.

Case summaries – for key cases. The short precis allows the user to decide whether a case is relevant to them. This is currently being expanded to cover High Court, House of Lords and ECJ cases.

Alerter – a weekly paper or e-mail bulletin summarising key cases recently approved. The Alerter can be circulated to all members of a firm or chambers and incorporated within a firm's own internal information systems and bulletins.

Case Detective offers assistance in locating cases – 'if you can't find it ... we will!' Contact us by telephone, fax or e-mail and we help identify the case you're looking for – then you can download it directly from the service. Or if you're waiting for a case to be approved or for judgment to be given we'll monitor progress and let you know as soon as it's available.

There are both Subscription and Pay as You Go options, designed to suit all sectors of the market – by individual or firm, unlimited access or by subject.

Contact Sarah Andrews on 020 7421 4027 or sarah.andrews@smithbernal.com.

Sweet & Maxwell

www.smlawpub.co.uk

Free services

Badger Alerter: Hundreds of documents are issued every day from Whitehall, Westminster and the judiciary announcing changes to legislation, new regulations, SIs, decisions, codes of practice and proposals for consultation. These are listed and abstracted each day including marked reinforcement or weakening of a legal concept.

Law Brief and Case Reports from the *Solicitors Journal*.

Electronic Newsletters including European Union News Online, Local Government Library Online and Planning Bulletin Online.

Lists from all the Crown Courts in England and Wales, published daily.

Case of the Week from Current Law and European Current Law.

Student section with case digests of special interest to students.

The Bar Directory, published with the General Council of The Bar.

Kimes International Law Directory – 650 law firms in 270 jurisdictions.

Online updates on *Internet Law and Regulation*, edited by Graham Smith of Bird & Bird, and *Year 2000: Law and Liability* by Susan Singleton.

Contact Sarah MacCann at webmaster@smlawpub.co.uk

Subscription services

CLI (Current Legal Information) on CD-ROM and Internet, provides a fully searchable source of references to cases, statutes, statutory instruments, law reports, legal articles and 'grey paper' – the information emanating daily from government departments including white, green and consultation papers and press releases.

CLI comprises seven inter-linked, fully searchable databases, with facilities to search by case, legislation, company or keyword. Subscribers receive a new, updated CD each month and have the option to access the internet service, updated on a daily basis. The databases include:

Current Law Cases: summaries and digests of all reported cases, dating back to 1947. Current Law Cases allows you to see the facts and outcome of a case at a glance, and have the option of clicking straight to other cited cases, relevant legislation or press reports.

Badger: a ready-made index to the mountains of public domain information of interest to the legal profession, including official publications, statutory instruments, guidance notes and press releases. Badger provides a brief summary of every piece of information, with details on where the full text may be located.

Legal Journals Index: an index to every significant legal journal article published since 1986. The Legal Journals Index covers over 400 journals – academic and practitioner titles – from the UK and Europe.

Financial Journals Index: an index to articles appearing in over 80 financial journals, dating back to 1992, covering the areas of banking, insurance and pensions and the wider financial services sector.

Current Law Case Citator: a quick, comprehensive guide to all case law, giving a full judicial history of each case, stating where a case has been considered, overturned, or simply even referred to in subsequent case decisions. Updated weekly.

Current Law Legislation Citator: showing where and how statutes and statutory instruments have been amended, considered or otherwise affected through subsequent legislation. Updated weekly.

Inns of Court catalogues showing the resources held in the libraries of the Middle and Inner Temples, Gray's Inn and Lincoln's Inn. Updated three times a year.

Contact Jane Atkins at Jane.Atkins@smlawpub.co.uk or 020 7449 1111 for a free trial.

Legal Research on the Internet

by James Behrens

Editors' preface

This review looks at the principal sources of UK legal research information on the internet. We are grateful to the publishers for providing passwords and also to James himself. The review took a great deal of time and it is clear that it could have gone on for ever and still not have been totally comprehensive and totally consistent! We would like to stress that it is just 'one person's review' and others may disagree with the relative virtues of the sites concerned.

These are almost all subscription-only services but most of the publishers will provide a free trial period if asked. It is well worth trying out some of the services for your particular needs before taking any decisions. (See www.venables.co.uk/legal/publish.htm for links.)

The publishers are described below in roughly the order in which James carried out the review:

- Sweet & Maxwell's Current Legal Information
- Lawtel
- Butterworths' Law Direct
- New Law Online
- Smith Bernal
- Justis Online (based on CDs) and Justis.com
- Lexis-Nexis
- The Incorporated Council of Law Reporting

Finally, we ask publishers not to quote from this review since comments taken out of the context of the whole article are almost certainly misleading!

Sweet & Maxwell's Current Legal Information

Sweet & Maxwell's Current Legal Information (CLI) on the internet is an extension to Sweet & Maxwell's CD-ROM service of the same name. The CLI is an extremely comprehensive source of material. It includes, for example, all cases reported in Current Law from 1947. The CD is updated monthly, and the main advantage of the Internet version is that it contains material which is not yet on the most recent CD. The internet material goes back to 1986.

I found the CLI to be a particularly easy site to use. It is possible to log on to it quickly and the layout is clear. I explored both the full text and field level search options, doing searches on each. The field level search is more specific, enabling one to search by case name, court, judge, legislation, scope, and cases mentioned. Somewhat surprisingly the two types of searches sometimes produced different results for the same material. For example, a search for 'barbrak' (a reference to *Kleinwort Benson v Barbrak Ltd* [1987] AC 597) as a full text search produced only one result, but the same word entered into the 'cases mentioned' field in a field level search produced 13 results, the latest being in 1998.

I compared these results with the same searches done using the CD software. A free text search for 'barbrak' on the CD produced 11 results. The reason for the discrepancy between the CD and the online service may be that the software is different, or it may be that the databases are not identical.

Another subject I wanted to research was the principle of non-derogation from grant in relation to leases. Entering 'non-derogation' in the full text search drew up one case; entering 'derogation from grant' produced four results. On the CD 'non derogation' produced 14 results, 'derogation from grant' produced 15 results.

I also wanted to research the principles governing the introduction of fresh evidence in the Court of Appeal. Entering 'fresh evidence and Court of Appeal', I found nine results on the online service, but 186 on the CD! The search limits were concise and helpful (indicating what Boolean operators were available) and the layout of the results was even better. It was possible to choose various result options, eg cases this month, cases with legislation, cases in chronological or reverse-chronological order.

Each case was listed with its various citations and a very fulsome description of the issues, similar to that above a headnote in a law report. It enabled me to see at a glance whether the case was relevant for my purposes. The cases were listed in small print and a different colour was used for name, citation and description. This made it incredibly easy to scan a large list of results very quickly and to find what I was looking for.

As a general source of reference I would not be without the CD service. I would not wish to use the internet service as a replacement for the CD service, but it is a worthwhile addition to it, and is very easy to use.

Lawtel

Although it was similarly quick to open and well laid out, Lawtel did not quite reach the high standard set by Current Legal Information. On searching for 'non--derogation' I found only two entries. Typing in 'derogation from grant' proved slightly more fruitful, showing 15 results. 'Fresh evidence and Court of Appeal' produced 245 results.

Although Lawtel produced a similar number of results on each search, the results are not as helpfully laid out as in Current Legal Information. A sentence or two is given on the issues in each case. However, the general descriptions/keywords are not as detailed: they do not always correspond to – and are usually more general than – the search entry. The print is larger and the information (eg case name, details, general description) is arranged vertically rather than horizontally. All this (though it may seem to be splitting hairs) actually makes the list of results much harder and slower to read. The search tips seem to be geared towards more general searches on a broad subject than particular phrases or keywords.

Finally, although Lawtel covers cases that would usually be found in specialist law reports, it covers cases from the main reports (WLR, All ER, official reports, etc) as far back only as 1980. This makes it less comprehensive than the Current Legal Information, but a useful site to check recent developments.

Lawtel enables one to search through statutory instruments for a particular text. A search for 'mediation' yielded five references. SIs from 1997 onwards contain hypertext links to the original versions of the full text on the HMSO website. This is a useful feature, but not as comprehensive as the legislation direct service on the Butterworths site, reviewed below.

Butterworths Law Direct

Law Direct is primarily a current awareness alerting service. It is not primarily a deep research tool to locate case materials. It provides daily summaries of cases and statutory material almost as soon as they are published. For example, on 27 July, it had reports of cases decided as recently as 23 July. Although the material was well summarised, I found the screens far from intuitive.

Of more interest to me than the daily update service was Law Direct's research capabilities, and here I have to report that Law Direct did not score highly in my estimation. The articles citator claims 'Contains details of all articles published in the major legal journals. Search the articles citator to locate any article published since the beginning of 1995.' The search found no articles written by me over this period, whereas by comparison Sweet & Maxwell's Current Legal Information CD lists seven.

Butterworths claims 'Our powerful search engine enables you to search across all the Practice Areas and customise your searches.' A search for 'barbrak' (a reference to *Kleinwort Benson v Barbrak Ltd* [1987] AC 597) produced the result in four seconds that the database had 4 records which mentioned the case. However to get to the first of these cases then took 37 seconds of waiting. The reason for this delay is that Butterworths sends a huge archive of cases to my screen, and then searches through that archive on my screen to get to the first search result. The start of the file appeared on my screen within six seconds, and there was no warning to tell me that the program was still working, and that I should wait for a full half minute for the rest of the file to be transferred to my screen. To get the second of the four cases on 'barbrak' a new archive file had to be sent, taking 25 seconds; to get the third case the wait was 34 seconds, and for the fourth case, 22 seconds.

The cases which Law Direct found were relevant, but did not include any 1999 cases. By way of comparison, the same search in New Law On Line quickly located 12 cases, including *Shapland v Palmer*, a Court of Appeal decision of 23 March 1999. Plainly for legal research New Law On Line is more comprehensive, more reliable, and easier to use. And for breadth of coverage Smith Bernal's Casetrack beats them both: a search for 'barbrak' located 16 cases, including *Shapland v Palmer* and two other cases in 1999 (see below).

On the positive side, there are hypertext links between the Law Direct databases and other services provided by Butterworths. So, for example, if you are a subscriber to Butterworths' All England Direct service, you can click on any All ER reference and the program will immediately take you to the full text of that report. If however you are not a subscriber to that service there is nothing to warn you that the All ER hypertext links are not operative, and you will be puzzled at the long pause which follows when you press on the link.

I found Butterworths' legislation direct service excellent. Here one can search through the text of all acts of parliament, statutory instruments and measures, to find, for example, all references to 'mediation': there are 118 of them, ranging from the Schedule 1 to the Antarctic Treaty Act 1967 to Schedule 1 to the Extradition (Drug Trafficking) Order 1997, with immediate access to the exact text of the legislation. Law Direct informed me that the Cathedrals Measure received the Royal Assent on 30 June 1999, and I was disappointed that as at 27 July the Legislation Direct service did not have the full text of this measure available; but apart from this I could not fault the service.

CCH New Law Online

I must come clean and say that my chambers subscribes to this service, and I use it regularly. It contains cases on Commercial, Property, Criminal/Divisional, Employment, Intellectual Property, Revenue Law, European Court of Justice areas, and is extremely useful. A search for 'measure of damages professional negligence property' yielded 53 results, including 5 in 1999, the most recent being 22 April (a fortnight before I am writing this review), and including one House of Lords decision, *Platform Home Loans Ltd v Oyston Shipways Ltd*, decided in February 1999. These cases are presented first as short five line summaries. A click leads to a fuller headnote on any particular case, a further click to the judgment itself.

In a case concerning whether the court would extend the validity of a claim form, I entered the word 'barbrak', a reference to *Kleinwort Benson v Barbrak Ltd* [1987] AC 597, a leading case in the area, and the search yielded 12 cases on the subject.

In most cases you can download the full judgment already formatted as a Word document with page numbering and copyright notice. Sometimes this feature did not work properly, and when this happened I saved the text of the judgment as it appeared on the screen onto my hard disk.

Smith Bernal

I have looked at this site over a period of three months, and it has been much improved over this period, partly as a result of feedback by myself to Smith Bernal. By the time this review is printed, the fault which I identify in this review will probably have been put right. I think it is right to refer to it none the less, first, to show the type of difficulty one can have when using a site, and second, to show Smith Bernal's good will and commitment to put right any problems when their attention is drawn to them.

The problem I had was when searching for cases referring to the decision *Kleinwort Benson v Barbrak Ltd.* First I selected High Court cases. I entered the word 'barbrak' in the 'casename' field, and the search yielded no results. I then tried leaving the 'casename' field blank, and entering the word 'barbrak' in the 'full text searching' field. Likewise, no results. I then did the same searches, having selected Court of Appeal cases. Entering 'barbrak' in the 'casename' field yielded no results. Entering it instead in the 'full text searching' field yielded 16 results. At last! The most recent case is an unreported Smith Bernal transcript of 11 May, two months before I am writing this review, and is precisely on the point I needed at the time.

The problem here is that the instructions did not make clear which field I should use for my search. They acknowledge this, and say that the fault will be put right.

As a comparison with other websites, I entered the search string 'measure of damages and professional negligence and property'. This yielded seven cases, all in 1998. This was not nearly as comprehensive as the same search in New Law Online.

Smith Bernal's strength is in its database of transcripts of judgments, and it is clear that if you handle the site correctly, you will strike gold. At the time I write it is easy for an inexperienced user to miss the gold that is there, but I expect Smith Bernal will soon provide clearer instructions on screen so that this is less likely to happen.

Justis Online

Justis Online acts as an extension to the CD-ROM service provided by Context. It provides access to cases reported after the release of the most recent CD. You do not access the service via the Internet, but you can set up your Justis software to operate the online service automatically whenever you use the CD. You enter your ID and password into one of the Justis software menu options, and in the 'select database' option you select the online databases you wish to connect to. Once this is set up, when you start the Justis software, your modem dials the connection number, and every search is then made on both the CD and the online database.

To see how the service worked I searched for a word which was likely to be in recent cases as well as on the CD. I searched for the word 'damages' in the key words field. This yielded 973 cases. The first seven on the results screen (the most recent) were marked with an asterisk, to show they were on the online database, rather than on the CD. Clicking on one of these produced the full text of the report, exactly as on the normal CD service. The integration of the CD and the online database really was, to use the jargon, seamless.

I tried a search for 'professional negligence and measure and damages and property'. This yielded 16 cases reported on the WLR CD, and *Platform Home Loans Ltd v Oyston Shipways Ltd*, now reported as [1999] 2 WLR 518, but not at the time of writing available on the WLR CD. A search for 'barbrak' yielded 22 cases, all on the WLR CD.

I use the Justis Electronic Law Reports and Weekly Law Reports regularly. This online service is a very useful addition and works perfectly.

Context publish several series of law reports on CD, including the Electronic Law Reports (ie the main series of law reports published by the Incorporated Council of Law Reporting), Lloyds Law Reports, the Weekly Law Reports, Industrial Cases, The Times Law Reports, Common Market Law Reports, Family Law Reports, and Criminal Appeal Reports. The Justis Online service, which is an extension to this service, and which is accessed using the Justis software supplied with the CDs, is reviewed above.

The new online service is accessed via the internet, and comprises the Electronic Law Reports, the Weekly Law Reports, the Law Reports Digest and the Times Law Reports.

The online service is very similar to the CD service. You select the databases you wish to search in (you can do searches across several databases at once), and you then come to the search screen where you enter the search information in the appropriate field. You can enter the search as free text (ie anywhere in the database), or can search in the fields for parties, catchwords, court, judge, judgment and year. The first field says 'To find a specific document, type in a document reference'. It was not obvious that instead of 'document reference', they mean 'case reference' . I tried entering a case reference 1998 Ch 482, and this worked perfectly.

I then entered 1999 AC 30, and the database found 1999 AC 1, which is the start of the case containing page 31, and I had to press page down several times to get to page 31. Similarly I entered 1999 AC 60, and the database found 1999 AC 54, which is the start of the case containing page 60.

A search for 'Beddoe' (a reference to *In re Beddoe* [1893] 1 Ch. 547, a well-known trust case), produced 42 references, listed on three pages. The cases in the Law Reports were listed first, followed by the cases in the Weekly Law Reports, followed by cases in The Times, in each list the most recent cases being shown first. Each case is given with its reference, a brief key-word description, and the case reference. A click on any reference took me to the report of the case. The case reports had hypertext links to other cases cited. In some cases there were hypertext links marked to other series of law reports not available through Context. For example, *Dagnell and Another v J L Freedman & Co. (a Firm)* reported in Times Law Reports for 12 March 1993, had a hypertext link marked to *Baly v Barrett* [1988] NI 368, a Northern Ireland series of reports not provided by Context.

Context may have done this so that the link is ready for use if Context do provide this series of reports in the future, but the program ought to disable hypertext links which are not yet operative, so that users do not try them.

There were a number of problems associated with printing. No printing facility is provided by the program, and the results obtained using the web browser's printing facility are quite unsuitable for citation in court. There was also a problem with the speed in which icons appeared on the screen, but the service is new, and these problems may have been put right by the time you read this.

The service is clearly designed to appear very similar to the CD service. It does contain more recent cases than are on the CD, but that apart I can see no justification for paying the full price for the service if you already take the CD.

Lexis-Nexis

I found using Lexis on the web both easy and effective. The same Boolean operators are used as in the proprietary Lexis software. So, for example, you can search for 'murphy pre/3 brentwood district council' ('murphy' within three words before 'brentwood district council') to find all cases which cite *Murphy v Brentwood DC* [1999] 1 AC 398. The search produced 65 results.

Search results are displayed on the screen 25 cases at a time. A list display gives the name of the case, the court, the date, whether the case was reported (and the report citation if it is), or whether it is available only as a transcript. A click on any case took me to the full report, and I was able to print the ones I wanted. You can choose an expanded list display which gives the line of the text which contained the search term. This was of no use in the case of my *Murphy v Brentwood DC* search, but when I searched in the English case law database for 'church w/15 dispute' ('church' within 15 words of 'dispute'), the expanded list printed the lines in the text of the reports which contained these words, and this gave me a clue as to what each report was about. This expanded list display is not nearly as full or as useful as the case summaries in Sweet & Maxwell's Current Legal Information, but it is better than nothing.

I was able to search through English statutes and statutory instruments, and go straight to the sections of the Acts containing the text I was searching for. There is nothing much to choose between searching statutory material using Lexis and using Butterworths Legislation Direct.

Some Lexis search commands are unlike those of any other search engine. For example in Lexis 'damag!' can be used to search for damage, damages, damaged, and damaging. Many users of other search engines are accustomed to using the asterisk, as in 'damag*', to carry out the same search. It seems a pity that Lexis has not yet been modified to bring its command structure in line with these other search engines. But apart from this quibble, the service is excellent.

I cannot leave this review without commenting how impressed I was with the material available on Lexis. I found here the full transcripts of several cases on judicial review which were not available in any other source, and I was particularly impressed with the database of newspaper reports and articles. Some of these are available on CD-ROM – the Inner Temple Library for example has a CD of articles in The Times – but nothing that I have seen beats Lexis' coverage of news. Research into the newspaper coverage of the dispute in 1998 between Dr Neary and the Dean and Chapter of Westminster Abbey, produced over 130 articles from 21 different newspapers.

The Incorporated Council of Law Reporting

Although the Incorporated Council of Law Reporting is good at reporting House of Lords cases quickly, many other important cases take months before they are reported. Looking for example at the Weekly Law Reports issue for 16 July 1999, I see a House of Lords decision from 1 July 1999 – excellent, a Privy Council decision and a decision by Lightman J both in March 1999 – fair, and a Court of Appeal decision from 6 November 1998 – appalling.

If Court of Appeal cases take over eight months to be reported, it is no wonder that practitioners need to look elsewhere for their material. The second problem with the Incorporated Council of Law Reporting is its choice of cases. Whereas ten to fifteen years ago, almost every case I cited in court was reported in the official Law Reports, now the proportion is far less than 50 per cent. Regularly I have to turn to cases on company law, housing law, insolvency, professional negligence, and property law, which are not reported in the official Law Reports. This does not simply reflect my own specialisms, but is true for many practitioners. There has been a proliferation of independent law reporting over the last fifteen years. It is as though we are going back to the good old days of nominate reports, before the official Law Reports series began in 1865.

So I approach a website which limits its material to providing summaries of cases which have been or are about to be published in the official Law Reports with two thoughts. First, I am pleased that the website will go some way to mitigating the appalling delay before important cases are published in the Law Reports. Even if they are not yet in the Law Reports, at least there are summaries of them on the Incorporated Council of Law Reporting website. (For example, on 20 July 1999 the website listed eight Court of Appeal cases decided in July, the latest being 16 July.) But, second, for any serious research, I need to use far more than just the official Law Reports.

The material on the website is well laid out, and is easy to use. It is also free! However, it lacks any form of search facility, and can hardly be described as comprehensive. It is impossible to see what cases there have been on, for example, professional negligence, without browsing through, first, House of Lords cases, second, Court of Appeal cases, third, Queen's Bench cases, and fourth, Chancery Division cases. At the time of writing (20 July 1999), there are no cases reported in this area on the site.

Clearly, as the material on the website increases, the website may start to have some use. However, until the Incorporated Council of Law Reporting addresses the fundamental problem of the choice of material it publishes, I will continue to look elsewhere for the material I need.

James Behrens is a barrister in general chancery and commercial litigation and advice. He is a council member of the Society for Computers and Law and he has written widely on computers in legal research, word processing and data protection. Contact James at Serle Court Chambers, Thirteen Old Square, Lincoln's Inn, London WC2A 3UA; telephone 020 7242 6105; email james.behrens@dial.pipex.com; website www.serlecourt.co.uk/cv/JB.htm

Publishers in Particular Areas of Law

Note that the general publishers described above may offer specialist services as well; this section just looks at those publishers who only provide services in a particular area of law.

Criminal Law Week

www.criminal-law.co.uk

Subscription service

Criminal Law Week is a weekly digest of all new developments in the criminal law, covering both case law and statute law, primary and subordinate. Commentary is provided by James Richardson, in practice for over 20 years at the criminal bar, and editor of *Archbold* for many years. Criminal Law Week online replicates the paper version, but is available sooner than the paper product and includes access to all back issues (the database now comprises 3,000 cases).

Contact James Richardson on 01483 414040 or james_richardson@criminal-law.co.uk.

DiscLaw Publishing – Employment Law

www.emplaw.co.uk

Subscription services

DiscLaw Publishing produces Employment Law on a Disc (e-LOAD), also marketed by The Law Society. The service is aimed at in-house lawyers and general legal practitioners (at a budget price) rather than just being an expert system for specialists. In addition to commentary, precedents and full text of the main employment law statutes e-LOAD includes direct links to ICR case reports on CD-ROM (in the Justis series produced by Context Ltd – see above).

e-LOAD is reissued at 6-monthly intervals and is supported by a 3-weekly web updating service. Instant 24 hour passwords are available online for £5 plus VAT.

Free services

More than 1,200 free pages of basic employment law information derived from a 1997 version of the program are available as well as an interactive UK map for locating solicitors with employment law expertise on the site. Law firms with employment law capability can apply for a free e-mail link (an extended entry can be obtained for a fee).

Contact Henry Scrope on 01235 833122 or disclaw@community.co.uk.

Jordan Publishing – Family Law

www.familylaw.co.uk

Free services

Family Law Update is a fast-track case reporting and practice news service, which contains summaries of cases, legislation and practice developments of interest to family law specialists. The archive has been built from the start of 1997, and new material is added weekly.

Users can access the most recent week's (or month's) material. Alternatively, they can view all items under a particular subject heading, or search through separate alphabetical listings of all case-law, legislation and practice items.

In addition, every word of every summary is indexed, so that a single word, or combination of words, can be searched across the whole database, or a particular subject area or just to case-law, legislation or practice items.

A set of links to websites of interest to family law practitioners and the Family Law Forum provides a discussion forum for professionals.

Subscription services

FamLex – Family Lawyers Library – Legislation Service. This provides bi-monthly CD-ROM updates of Family Law statutes with online access with weekly updates to legislation available online. The service is offered free to all subscribers of Hershman & McFarlane: Children Law and Practice on CD and the Family Court Practice on CD.

Civil Court Service – tri-annual CD updates of the new Civil Procedures Rules, with Practice Directions and 'fillable' and printable forms. Regularly updated website and opt-in email notification of changes to the Rules available to subscribers at www.civilcourtservice.co.uk.

Contact Ros Young, 0117 918 1242 or ryoung@jordanpublishing.co.uk.

Legalease – International Centre for Commercial Law

www.icclaw.com

Legalease has been a pioneer of online legal services, first with the Legal Information Network (LINK), launched in 1994, and subsequently with the International Centre for Commercial Law, the web home of the influential Legal 500 Series featuring recommendations for law firms and lawyers in the UK, US, Europe, Asia Pacific and Middle East. This is one of the largest and most comprehensive legal sites outside the US with over 60,000 pages.

Free services

The Legal 500 series of publications (as just described).

UK and European Commercial Law updates, with contributions from some of The UK and Europe's leading law firms.

LASER – a fully searchable directory of law firm websites worldwide.

The Courts & Agency Directory – a comprehensive guide to law firms undertaking agency work in The UK.

The Legal Experts Directory – a fully searchable guide to over 1,500 of the leading legal lights in the UK.

International Legal News – key stories from the world of commercial law updated every weekday.

The Student Law Centre – extensive details of law firms offering training contracts and holiday placements and chambers offering pupillages and mini-pupillages. There is also information about law schools, an editorial section produced in collaboration with a range of law firms, advice about preparing a curriculum vitae and a 'behind the scenes' look at training at different law firms and barristers chambers.

Subscription service

IT+Communications Law Journal (ITCLJ) is a comprehensive source of information on how the law is coping with the digital revolution. The material comes in a combination of printed law reports, a newsletter, a disk of the material and a subscribers-only website.

Contact Neil Evans at 020 7396 9309 or neil.evans@link.org.

Electronic Immigration Network (ein)

www.ein.org.uk

Free services

Links to immigration-related sites worldwide, and an events listing.

Subscription services

Full text of Immigration Tribunal determinations, continuously updated with the most recent cases and indexed with more than 800 keywords. The database can also be searched by full text, date, court, judge, location and decision. The database contains over 3,000 Immigration Tribunal determinations and other case reports and summaries from the higher courts. The tribunal determinations represent the core material of current jurisprudence on immigration and asylum law.

The ein database is now used by a growing number of immigration tribunal adjudicators and all immigration practitioners are advised to consider membership to the project.

Contact Jocelyn Manners-Armstrong on 01706 759520 or ein-admin@ein.org.uk.

Medical-Legal Information Service

www.medneg.com

This is the online version of the journal *Medical Litigation*.

Free services

Newsbriefs provides a monthly review of medico-legal developments.

Subscription services

There is access to case reports, articles from the journal, abstracts of articles from other medical journals, settlements in medical negligence cases, High Court writs and Parliamentary questions and answers, all of which can be downloaded. Subscribers can also download the 1998 Medical Litigation Index which lists over 1,500 case summaries, including selected Australian, Canadian and United States decisions.

Contact Charlie Roberts at enquiries@medneg.com or 0800 328 5019.

Estates Gazette Interactive (EGi) – Property Law Service

www.propertylaw.co.uk

This is an online news and information service for law professionals working in the property market. The service is used by over 750 property and planning lawyers, barristers and information managers from over 200 firms. It was the winner of the Best Business Publishing website award at the 1998 New Media Age Effectiveness Awards.

Daily Property Law News covers court decisions, government announcements, financial and legal business and issues in property and planning law. Property Market News for company and property market information, updated hourly throughout the day from EGi.

Full text of Estates Gazette Law Reports since 1975. Forthcoming Estates Gazette Law Reports for future issues of the Estates Gazette magazine. Full text of Estates Gazette Planning Law Reports since 1988. Full text Estates Gazette Case Summaries updated daily and archived since 1988.

Archive of the full text of key articles from the Estates Gazette since 1986.

Who's Who in Property: profiles of over 7,000 professionals. Who's Suing Whom? A selection of property and planning writs.

Legislation Database.

Also, Parliamentary Watch, Lands Tribunal Database, environmental risk assessment checking, reference bookshop and a diary of events.

Register on site for a free trial.

Other Publisher Websites

Links to other publisher websites are at www.infolaw.co.uk/ifl/publish.htm

In addition to the sites featured above, all other publishers with significant law or law-related lists have websites providing access to information about their publications. Many include the facility to order their publications online and most provide at least some useful free information services.

Barry Rose publish practical legal textbooks.

Blackstone Press is a long-established legal publisher with over 400 student and practitioner titles.

Blackwells Some law publishing. Web resource centres and mailing lists for several categories (Business and Finance to follow).

Cambridge University Press has a substantial law list.

Cameron May are environmental and trade law publishers.

Carlton Group publishes government guides and directories.

Cavendish Publishing are academic, professional and Australian law publishers; law links.

CCH Editions Limited publish Personnel Management, Commercial and Company Law, Taxation, Insolvency and Auditing titles.

Chambers and Partners produce legal directories and magazines.

Delia Venables In addition to her legal resources pages, Delia provides a web tutorial and guided tour and information from the Internet Newsletter.

Gee Publishing has a free discussion forum, business directories and job listings and chargeable databases of business and finance documents, articles and customisable news updates.

Globefield Press produce international trade law publications.

HLT Publications is a division of Holborn College and produce student law publications.

HMSO publish the full text of statutes since January 1996; SIs from January 1997 (see p 52).

Incomes Data Services are publishers of emploment law, pay analysis and human resources management materials.

Informa Professional Publishing (formerly LLP Limited) are principally focused on shipping, insurance, and maritime and commercial law.

Information for Lawyers Limited provides comprehensive web indexes to web lawyers, legal resources and lawtech and a Civil Procedure Rules service.

Kluwer Law International is an international law publisher, part of Wolters Kluwer NV.

Law Pack produce do-it-yourself legal publications which enable users to handle their own straightforward legal transactions.

Mondaq offers global coverage of legislation and regulations, corporate finance, offshore finance, market analysis, economic analysis, risk management, property, consultancy, and worldwide business news.

Monitor Press Ltd produce legal and business publications.

OUP Law publish abstracts from many OUP law journals on the web.

Perpetuity Press are criminal law publishers.

PLC Publications publish practical law and legal information for business lawyers.

The Stationery Office Ltd publish online versions of Parliamentary publications including Hansard, Lords judgments, Bills in Progress and the weekly information bulletin (see further p 54).

Tolley Publishing are tax publishers now part of Butterworths.

Waterlow publish online versions of their law directories.

Chapter 5

Legal Resources by Topic

Contents

This chapter is intended to serve as an index to the most useful UK websites in particular areas of law and practice *offering free access*, with a brief description of each site. Note that the law publishers' subscription services are not generally referred to – see Chapter 4 for full details of their services.

The essence of the index is selectivity. We do not seek to score points by listing all the URLs we know: that would be counter-productive; rather the sites mentioned have been selected as meeting one of the following criteria:

- Sites which provide a good jumping-off point for research on that topic: These sites generally contain a focussed selection of links to other sites and often provide also useful content such as news and articles.

- Sites which provide a substantial information resource on that topic: These services may be provided by universities, law firms, or commercial publishers.

- Sites of relevant Government departments, governing organisations and professional associations: These are likely to prove reliable and useful resources – if not already, then in the future. Further details of these sites will be found in Chapter 2.

The focus is on *UK law and practice* sites. Thus, for example, you will not find listed many otherwise excellent sites where UK references are submerged beneath waves of US references. (International legal resource sites are covered in Chapter 13.) Though the focus is on sites with legal content, we have referred to some key business, financial and other industry information sites where we think they would be useful to a lawyer researching a particular topic.

Topics A–Z

*Links to sites mentioned are at www.infolaw.co.uk/ifl/law.htm
and www.venables.co.uk/legal/sites.htm*

This listing is based on Nick's Topics pages at www.infolaw.co.uk/ifl/law.htm. Delia's pages, at www.venables.co.uk/legal/sites.htm provide a broader set of headings, such as 'Business, Commercial, Financial and Corporate Resources, including Competition' rather than separate headings for the constituent parts. Thus, if you are looking for a particular topic it may be worth first looking at the detailed headings in Nick's pages, but then, if you cannot find what you want, trying also the more general headings on Delia's pages.

ADR and arbitration

ADR Group – Specialist mediation provider.

Centre for Alternative Dispute Resolution – Leading international body.

Chartered Institute of Arbitrators – Professional body whose object is to promote and facilitate the determination of disputes by ADR.

International Chamber of Commerce: International Court of Arbitration – Rules and awards of the ICC International, Court of Arbitration.

London Court of International Arbitration – Comprehensive international dispute resolution service.

Arts

Institute of Art and Law – A small independent organisation aiming to bridge the divide between the worlds of art and law; includes links and online articles.

Aviation

Aeronet – Information resource for the commercial air transport sector.

Banking

Bank of England.

Silkscreen Publishing: Money Laundering Compliance Website – Resource for professionals in law, banking and financial services. There are pages on the detection and prevention of fraud, details of conferences and seminars, book reviews and a large collection of links.

Building and construction

Construction Industry Computing Association – Impartial advice, information and consultancy to those in all parts of the construction industry, its clients and those supplying systems to it.

Corbett & Co – Specialist construction law firm; site includes discussion forum and links.

Court Service: Technology and Construction Court – Judgments, practice directions, daily lists and notices.

Masons: Construction and Engineering – Online Construcion Law Reports, articles, Guide to EC Law, brochures, newsflashes and a useful set of links.

Society of Construction Law – Information related to the construction industry and links to relevant sites of interest.

Winward Fearon: Construction Briefings – Online newsletter and articles.

Business and finance

CAROL – Blue chip company annual reports online

Evening Standard.

Financial Services Authority.

Financial Times.

FIND: financial information net directory.

Gee Business Network – Business compliance information service, covering human resources, company administration, payroll and health & safety issues.

London Stock Exchange.

Mondaq Business Briefing – Monitors the legislative and regulatory framework affecting business and investment in the UK and European Union, Eastern Europe, North America, South-East Asia & China, Africa and the Middle East and major offshore centres.

MoneyWorld – Just about all the money facts and links you need.

NASDAQ.

Strathclyde University: Business Information Sources on the Internet – Selective guide to sites which contain business information, with emphasis on UK sources. Maintained by Sheila Webber.

Charities

Charity Choice – Comprehensive charities database.

Charity Commission – Including the Register of Charities, detailing all 180,000 registered charities in England and Wales, updated daily.

Civil liberties

Campaign for Freedom of Information – Campaigns against unnecessary secrecy and for a Freedom of Information Act.

Freedom of Information Unit – Carries out the development of the Government's policy.

Civil procedure

See also Court Practice and Procedures, p 57.

2 Temple Gardens: Woolf Commentary.

Beagle: Civil Procedure Rules – The new Rules and related materials including recent Costs PD and a slideshow; navigate using the framed contents lists and links or use the search facility using simple search terms or Boolean expressions.

Butterworths: Woolf Tracking Service – Book extracts, articles, annotated text of the new rules and practice directions.

Civil Justice Council – Established under the Civil Procedure Act 1997, the Council's remit is to: keep the civil justice system under review; consider how to make the civil justice system more accessible, fair and efficient; advise the Lord Chancellor and the judiciary on the development of the civil justice system.

Court Service – Judgments, practice directions and daily lists and forms and leaflets in pdf format.

Horne, Roger: Yet Another Woolf Site – The Rules with added value hypertext links.

LawOnLine: Woolf in Force – Authored by Laurie West-Knights, providing commentary on primary sites covering the Civil Procedure Rules; updated daily.

Lord Chancellor's Department: Civil Matters – The Lord Chancellor's foreword, the Civil Procedure Rules, Practice Directions, a Glossary, the Schedules (ie surviving parts of the RSC/CCR), Pre-action Protocols, a link to the Forms page on the Court Service site.

Simmons & Simmons: The Woolf Reforms – Succinct commentary.

Sweet & Maxwell: The White Book – Cursory coverage aimed at White Book subscribers.

Watmores: The Woolf Reforms – Guidance for insurers on Woolf reforms.

Commercial

See also under more detailed headings.

Court Service: Commercial Court – Judgments, practice directions, daily lists and notices.

International Centre for Commercial Law – The Legal 500 and Lawyers in Europe database online.

Companies

Companies House – Including free searches of disqualified directors and companies name and address index with basic company information.

Court Service: Companies Court – Judgments, practice directions and daily lists.

RM Online – Company information, formations and searches; trade mark registration and searches.

Institute of Chartered Secretaries and Administrators – Including publications and useful links.

Computer and communications

British Computer Society – Exists to provide service and support to the IS community, including individual practitioners, employers of IS staff and the general public.

CCTA – The aim of CCTA, the Central Computer and Telecommunications Agency, is to improve the delivery of public services by the best use of information technology.

Court Service: Technology and Construction Court – Judgments, practice directions, daily lists and notices.

Federation Against Software Theft – Summary of copyright law relating to software and information for industry, professionals and the public.

Journal of Information, Law and Technology – Leading electronic law journal covering a range of topics relating to IT law and applications.

Masons: Computer Law Reports – Commentaries and headnotes of computer law cases from July 1994 to date.

Society for Computers and Law – Including discussion groups, links and the online version of Computers & Law magazine.

Constitution

International Association of Constitutional Law – Forum for the exchange of knowledge and information and the development of understanding of constitutional systems.

Consumer

Office of Fair Trading – Including Fair Trading magazine and links.

Trading Standards Central – One stop shop for consumer protection information, maintained by the Institute of Trading Standards Administration.

Trading Standards Net – Jazzy commercial site which includes a wealth of consumer law resources, including links and legislation.

Copyright

See also Intellectual property

Copyright Licensing Agency – Including a summary of copyright law.

HMSO: Copyright Unit – Information about Crown copyright and HMSO licensing policy.

HMSO: The Future Management of Crown Copyright – A blueprint for the future management of Crown copyright which caters not only for the needs of business and professional and specialist interest groups, but also for the citizen.

The Copyright Website – (US) 'Endeavors to provide real world, practical and relevant copyright information of interest to infonauts, netsurfers, webspinners, content providers, musicians, appropriationists, activists, infringers, outlaws, and law abiding citizens.'

Courts and cases

Court Service – Selected judgments, practice directions, court lists, notices, forms and leaflets.

Europa: European Court: Recent Judgments – Searchable database of recent judgments of the Court of Justice and of the Court of First Instance.

Incorporated Council of Law Reporting: Daily Law Notes – Free headnotes of selected High Court judgments.

Lord Chancellor's Department – Wide range of information and links concerned with the administration of justice; plus the Civil Procedure Rules.

Northern Ireland Court Service.

Scottish Courts Website.

Smith Bernal: Casebase – Free database of archived (previous year back) AC judments since April 1996; Casetrack is a subscription service providing added value.

The Stationery Office: House of Lords Judgments – Since 14 November 1996.

Swarbrick: Case Index – index of case reports since 1992 which can be searched by keyword as well as date and court.

The Times: Law Reports.

Criminal

Criminal Cases Review Commission – Independent body responsible for investigating suspected miscarriages of criminal justice in England, Wales and Northern Ireland.

Criminal Justice System – Comprises the crime related work of criminal justice departments, and the agencies and services they oversee; links to theses sites.

Criminal Law Week – Weekly digest of developments in the criminal law; on subscription.

Howard League for Penal Reform – Independent charity working for humane and effective reform of the criminal justice and penal system in England and Wales; provides links.

King's College, London: Centre for Crime and Justice Studies – Well-classified links to: general criminal justice, criminology, law, media, police, prison (corrections), probation, research tools.

King's College, London: Coroner's Law Resource – Information, and links to information, relating to coroners' law and practice; compiled by Paul Matthews.

Lord Chancellor's Department: Criminal Matters; Magistrates

Magistrates Association – Information on vocation and training, plus links.

Penal Lexicon – Provides information on all matters concerned with prisons and penal affairs; by subscription; with extensive links.

Prisons Handbook – Sample chapters and a links library.

Serious Fraud Office – Investigates and prosecutes serious and complex fraud; includes case notes.

Sweet & Maxwell: Court Alerting Service – Court listings for Crown and High Court, using information from the Crown Court Electronic Support System (CREST).

UN Crime and Justice Information Network – Includes links to UN documents, UN and other organizations, statistical sources, country information, laws, treaties and constitutions.

University of Cambridge: Institute of Criminology – Includes links.

University of Edinburgh: Centre for Law and Society – Research in criminology and jurisprudence.

University of Glamorgan: Criminology and Criminal Justice – Resources.

University of Kent at Canterbury: Criminal Justice Links – Maintained by Steve Uglow.

University of Leeds: Criminal Justice Studies – Lectures, conferences and library resources; maintained by Clive Walker.

Data protection

Data Protection Public Register – Complete copy of the public register, updated weekly.

Data Protection Registrar – Guide and texts of all legislation and other documents.

Employment

CCH: Employment Law Legislation Tracker – With Lovell White Durrant; in-force and upcoming employment legislation and summaries of the law.

Commission for Racial Equality – Including a summary of the Race Relations Act.

Daniel Barnett – Mailing list for employment lawyers, with over 270 subscribers.

Emplaw: UK Employment Law on the Internet – Over 1,500 pages of free employment information plus employment lawyer directory etc.

Employment Appeal Tribunal – Judgments indexed by type of case, appellant, respondent or judge.

Federation of European Employers – Including legal sources and links.

Health and Safety Executive.

Incomes Data Services – Emploment law, pay analysis and human resources management resources and links.

Energy

Centre for Energy, Petroleum and Mineral Law and Policy – CEPMLP is part of the Faculty of Law and Accountancy at the University of Dundee.

Entertainment

Harbottle & Lewis – Wide range of articles on entertainment, media, (including newer industries such as digital mixed media), leisure and travel.

Environment

Best Environmental Directories – large database of environmental and environmental law links, supported by the Belgian Government.

Environmental Data Services Ltd – News and reports (subscription service).

Environmental Law Association – Aims to encourage collaboration between all those concerned with environmental law; collate and disseminate information; and identify, review, advise and comment on issues of environmental law and its application.

Information for Industry – Environment business magazines and manuals.

Institute for Global Communications: Environmental Law around the World – Links to treaties and other environmental law resources.

International Institute for Sustainable Development – Resource for environment and development policy makers.

Pace Virtual Environmental Law Library – Links to primary legal resources on environmental law.

United Nations Environment Programme – Treaties, programmes and links.

University of Indiana Virtual Law Library – Index of environmental law links.

University of Western Australia: Environmental Law – Selected links.

Family

1 Mitre Court Buildings – News.

Association of Child Abuse Lawyers – Practical support for lawyers and other professionals working for adults and children who have been abused.

Court Service: Family Division.

Court Service: Social Security and Child Support Commissioners.

Family Law Consortium – Articles, updates and links.

Family Mediators Association.

Jordans' Family Law – Includes case summaries.

Lord Chancellor's Department: Family Matters.

NCH Action For Children/Solicitors Family Law Association: Carelaw – Information site for young people in care in England and Wales, covering topics from rights in care to what happens after leaving care; given in a question and answer format.

Food

University of Reading, Department of Food Science & Technology: Food Law Pages – Prepared to assist students taking courses in food Law at the University of Reading. Maintained by Dr David Jukes.

Health

See also Mental health

Evans, David: Health Care – Newsletter and links.

Human rights

1 Crown Office Row: Human Rights Act and Update – Covers the Human Rights Act, Human Rights Convention and Strasbourg law.

Beagle: ECHR Website – Summaries of and extracts from EHCR cases; extracts from more important decisions; links to Strasbourg judgments; full HUDOC database.

DIANA – One of the oldest and most comprehensive databases of links on human rights topics.

European Court of Human Rights – General information, pending cases, judgments and decisions, basic texts and press releases.

Human Rights Web – Introduction, documents, and links to resources.

University of Essex: Human Rights Centre.

Immigration

BCL Immigration Services – Commercial site with immigration guides for individuals, companies and staff.

Electronic Immigration Network – Charity concerned with immigration, refugees and nationality law; comprehensive links to immigration and human rights issues.

Immigration Advisory Service – Large and experienced charity offering advice and representation in immigration and asylum matters.

Immigration Appellate Authority – Large library of links, statistics, a guide and addresses.

Immigration Law Practitioners' Association – Professional association of lawyers and academics concerned with immigration, asylum and nationality law.

Insolvency

Insolvency Service – Ofiicial Receiver addresses, statistics, guidance material; forms; complaints procedure; the competitiveness White Paper; the Civil Procedure Rules; disqualified directors hotline.

Society of Practitioners of Insolvency – Resources, links and a directory of practitioners.

UK Bankruptcy & Insolvency Website – Commercial website including data on businesses for sale, creditors meetings, liquidations, receiverships and administrations, and dividend announcements; a summary of the various insolvency options under the 1986 Act; and an Insolvency Update.

Insurance

Beachcroft Stanleys – Insurance Litigation Alert email newsletter.

Forum of Insurance Lawyers – Publications, contacts, news & dates, useful links and links to members' sites and a list of experts.

Insurolaw – Europe-wide network of insurance lawyers; includes Insurolaw Monitor – a trilingual newsletter on European legal/insurance issues.

Intellectual property

See also Copyright

Chartered Institute of Patent Agents – Basic information and advice, directory of patent agent firms, notices and comments, briefing papers and links.

Court Service: Patents Court.

European Patent Office – Official information and communications plus invitation to tender and abstracts of decisions of the Boards of Appeal with decsions available in pdf format.

Federation Against Software Theft (FAST) – Includes a summary of copyright law relating to software, information and news.

Institute of Trade Mark Agents – Including links to trade mark offices and organisations around the world and trade mark attorney websites; summaries of and links to recent decisions.

Intellectual Property Magazine – Leading US online magazine, including case digests, directory (of US practitioners) and links.

Intellectual Property Network – Free access to the more than 2 million US patents issued since 1971, and images of all US patents issued after 1974. An additional 1.4 million documents are available as PCT application data from WIPO and ESPACE-EP-A and ESPACE-EP-B from the EPO.

IPR-Helpdesk – Comprehensive information on IP; links to hundreds of IP-related websites; access to patent search systems such as the EPO's esp@cenet service; front ends to patent search services; and a document collection including national laws and EU Directives.

Kuesterlaw – Created and maintained by Jeffrey R Kuester, KuesterLaw is reportedly the most linked-to intellectual property website on the internet with law summaries and links.

Patent Office – All decisions issued by the Patent Office since 1998 and selected historical decsions, plus patent, trade mark and design and forms in pdf format.

Pipers: Patent & Trade Mark Attorneys – Worldwide listing.

University of Edinburgh: Shepherd and Wedderburn Centre for Research into IP and Technology – Includes a large selection of links.

Williams Powell & Associates – Specialist medium-sized practice; the site provides guidance and information for UK inventors and companies and for professionals throughout the world.

World Intellectual Property Organization – A host of resources and links.

International law

See also Marine

Auburn, Professor Francis, University of Western Australia: Public International Law – A collection of links on international law topics, linking to all major and topical issues.

Cornell University: International Court of Justice Homepage – Texts of the official judgments, advisory opinions, and orders which are received directly from the International Court of Justice.

Fletcher School of Diplomacy, Tufts University: Multilaterals Project – Covering atmosphere and space, flora and fauna – biodiversity, cultural protection, diplomatic relations, general, human rights, marine and coastal, other environmental, trade and commercial relations, rules of warfare, arms control, gulf area borders.

Internet

Clifford Chance: The Internet: Identifying And Managing Legal Risks Online – Online publication.

Cyber Rights and Cyber Liberties – Promotes free speech and privacy on the internet and raises public awareness of these important issues.

Electronic Commerce Association – Includes database of suppliers, case studies and a full glossary of terms, as well as links to other resources that may be able to help those with particular requirements.

Information Society Web Ring: Electronic Commerce Site – Including coverage of legal aspects, projects and actions, clusters, national initiatives, publications, events diary and links

Internet Law & Policy Forum – A neutral forum for developing solutions to legal and policy questions; working groups include self-regulation, digital signature, content blocking and certificate authorities.

Law Journal Extra: Law of the Internet – Glitzy online mag.

University of Berkeley, California: The Information Economy – Links.

Legal aid

Legal Aid Board.

Lord Chancellor's Department: Legal Aid.

Scottish Legal Aid Board.

Librarianship

Ariadne – Online magazine which describes and evaluates sources and services available on the web of use to librarians and information professionals; reports on developments in the Electronic Libraries Programme.

British and Irish Association of Law Librarians – Including useful links for law librarians and information professionals.

BUBL Information service: BUBL LINK – Catalogue of selected internet resources.

Marine

Council on Ocean Law – Conventions, commentaries, US positions, resources, issues and links.

Court Service: Admiralty Court.

Elbourne Mitchell – Case reports and commentary on re-insurance, shipping and regulatory matters.

Lloyd's Register.

Shoosmiths & Harrison: Marine Law Unit.

Medical negligence

Medneg.com – Online journal of medical negligence; cases to download, directories of relevant barristers, solicitors and medical experts.

Mental health

European Institute of Mental Health – Includes a discussion forum and links.

Hyperguide: Mental Health Act – Mental Health Act 1983 text and guidance.

Institute of Mental Health Law – Mental Health Act 1983 and allied legislation and case summaries.

Military

Aspals: Military law – Comprehensive links to relevant legislation, papers and reports, plus case notes.

Personal Injury

See also Insurance, Medical negligence

Association of Personal Injury Lawyers – Information, links and consultation papers.

Motor Accident Solicitors Society – Members directory and links.

Property and conveyancing

HM Land Registry – Information on property price reports, the Direct Access service, areas served, regional offices, lodging applications, fees; wide range of explanatory leaflets and reports in pdf.

Party Wall Resources Site – All you need to know and more about party walls.

Self help

Adviceguide – Basic advice and information on personal rights.

LawRights – Free independent legal information for the public (England & Wales)

National Association of Citizens Advice Bureaux – Directory and links to local CABs.

Taxation

Chartered Instutute of Taxation – Extensive information and links for the tax beginner and expert.

Gray's Inn Chambers: Tax Reporting Service – Case reports and links.

HM Treasury.

Inland Revenue.

UK Taxation Directory – Comprehensive links to tax-related sites, including indexes by source, by subject, international links and an email directory of tax professionals.

Trade

See also International law.

GATS Info Point – Guide to the General Agreement on Trade in Services, news and links.

Hieros Gamos: Guide to Global Trade Law – A comprehensive set of links in the following categories: supranational, national regimes, other resources, discussion groups, publications, related practices.

International Chamber of Commerce – ICC Guidelines, codes and rules for all areas of international business; rules and awards of the ICC International, Court of Arbitration.

International Trade Law Monitor – International/transnational commercial law and e-commerce infrastructure monitor, providing a huge number of links.

United Nations Commission on International Trade Law.

World Trade Organisation – Legal texts and thousands of WTO working documents, panel and appeals reports, new WTO agreements; meetings and conferences: summaries and documents, issues and documents dealing specifically, with developing countries.

Trusts and estates

Fungible Trust Website – All about fungible trusts, forms and precedents and a wide range of articles and examples.

Society of Trust and Estate Practitioners – Including a newsletter and technical update and tax digest.

Welfare

See also Self help

Department of Social Security – Comprehensive information plus publications and leaflets in pdf.

Ferret Information Systems – Benefits, housing and social work info and links; WeBenefits online magazine.

Heggs, Danny: Web Information Resources for Social Workers – Links.

Law Centres Federation – Encourages the development of publicly funded legal services for those most disadvantaged in society; includes newsletter and links.

Legal Action Group – National, independent charity which campaigns for equal access to justice for all members of society; includes info on publications, courses, useful contacts and links for all areas of social welfare.

Rathfelder, Martin: Weasel Words – Links to disability benefits sites; Incapacity Digest Online.

RightsNet – Designed to provide up to date social security information and news for advice workers; news, reviews, discussion and links.

Social Security and Child Support Commissioners – Forms, decisions and links.

Chapter 6

Finding Things on the Web

Contents

Search Engines

Few people other than information professionals and other web technofiles like using search engines. Users want to find things on the web quickly and easily. They are not interested in how the data is gathered, indexed or delivered, simply in the results themselves.

Search mechanisms are ubiquitous on the web. The term 'search engine' is most commonly understood to refer to the global search mechanisms which seek to index the whole of the web, but it should also be understood to encompass facilities with more modest aspirations: similar technologies are used to index information stored on local servers or groups of servers.

Global searches

Back in early 1995 it was estimated that there were 7 million pages on the web. This seemed, even at the time, to be a serious underestimate. Nevertheless a database of that order of magnitude was a formidable challenge for the search engines which grew up to service it. Four years on the web consists of probably more than a billion pages of information and an elite handful of services, including such names as **Alta Vista**, **Excite**, **Infoseek**, **Lycos** and **Yahoo**, have established themselves as robust and efficient solutions to searching the whole of the web (though none indexes every page).

Which search engine to use comes down in the end to personal preference. **Alta Vista** at www.altavista.com, consistently has the largest number of pages indexed, and the detail below is based on its functions. Other major search engines will provide similar functions.

Simple searches

Most people who use these sophisticated search tools use them in a very unsophisticated way, simply typing in a few words and hoping for the best. If you're one of this 80 per cent, bear in mind four simple points:

- Think before you type. Understand that you are searching a database which can contain literally anything: where 'case' does not mean just court proceedings, but 12 bottles of wine, travel goods, patient or client records etc. Understand also that you are searching web 'pages' which may be anything from a few to many hundreds of lines long.

- Get the basics right! Typing in a series of words will match any one or more of those words. Typing a phrase within "double quotes" will match that exact phrase. Generally use lower case only; use Initial Capitals only where you wish to restrict your search to instances of capitals.

- Interpret the results. Don't just click on the first titles you see. Assess the list for relevance according to the information provided: usually title, date and URL, and maybe summary as well. Refine or revise your search rather than ploughing through a long list of hits.

- Print out the Help pages. You may never read them otherwise.

Advanced searches

An advanced Alta Vista search

Once you are comfortable with the basics, why not read those Help pages you printed out? You're now into the world of advanced searches where formidable terms, like 'Boolean operators', once the preserve of information professionals, crop up.

Boolean operators or simply 'operators' are essentially the words AND, OR, NOT and NEAR – or their syntactical equivalent – used to connect search terms, thus refining the results. It should be obvious what each does on its own, but always bear in mind that the record being searched is a whole web page, so AND will bring back a page if the words occur anywhere in that page; they need not be near each other or connected in any way.

The operator NEAR is useful – broadening a search term (by finding terms within 10 words of each other) where one cannot afford to be too precise, but much more precise and useful than AND.

Operators and search terms can be combined in as many ways as you can imagine, and wildcards can also be used with word stems, but here you do need to read those Help pages again and develop your expertise further.

Searching fields and properties

html – the markup language for pages on the web – was originally designed to convey some structural information about the content of pages (eg there are tags for address blocks, defined terms and definition of those terms). However, it is essentially now used as a simple formatting language. There are thus no specific content-related fields which can be searched: you are searching the entire contents of each page.

However, there do exist for each page on the web, certain references and properties outside of its content which may be useful for search purposes and there is a particular syntax to enable you to do so. These are:

- the date of the page
- the title of the page (which appears in the title bar of most browsers)
- the URL of the page
- the domain of the site (ie .com, .org, .uk etc)
- the host computer for the site (eg www.bigco.com)
- the text of hyperlinks
- Java applets (programs)
- the filenames of images
- URLs of links on the page

Results

The results of your search will usually be displayed as a list of matches (hits) comprising:

- the title of the page, with a hypertext link to the page
- the URL
- the date of the page
- perhaps a brief extract or summary

Usually hits are listed in order of relevance, as determined by the frequency of occurrence of the search terms you have used and the exactness with which the combinations of terms have been matched.

Clearly, rather than working through the links in the list one by one, you need to review the list and decide whether to follow up some of the links offered or whether it is necessary to refine your current search.

Note that the title of a page is not the 72 point Arial bold title at the top of the page announcing 'The Widget Co', but the wording which appears in the title bar at the top of your browser's window. Hopefully, this should also announce 'The Widget Co', or if you are viewing a sub-page, perhaps 'The Widget Co: 1999 price list'. But it is surprising how many web pages omit a title altogether (in which case the URL is displayed) or comprise a title which out of context is meaningless (eg 'Products', 'Introduction' or – the worst of them all – 'Home Page' or 'Welcome').

If the title (and summary) are not of much help – and they often won't be – the URL will usually identify or give a clue to the name of the author or organisation as well as the country of publication and other details. For example www.widgetco.co.uk/products/pricelist.htm is clearly the price list for a UK company called Widget Co or similar; ourworld.compuserve.com/homepages/kthompson may well be the home page of your friend Keith Thompson and so on.

The date of a web page is of course useful if you are seeking out any sort of information which is time critical or where the date of publication has a particular significance. It is also a useful way of identifying pages which may be redundant or dormant. Dated pages will also point out those sites which are not updated as frequently as you would expect and hence may be of less value than would otherwise appear.

Local searches

Similar technologies are commonly employed to index and enable you to search local websites or groups of sites. Clearly if you are looking for information originating from a specific source, then the quickest route will be to visit that site and use the search engine provided there. For example the **CCTA Government Information Service** at www.open.gov.uk provides a search facility across all Government servers. Searching individual websites is often unrewarding unless they do contain large quantities of hard information. If the structure of the site is any good, it will usually be quicker to find the appropriate page by browsing.

Searching for things legal

Although there are search sites offering specifically legally-oriented searches, such as **FindLaw** at www.findlaw.com, these are heavily US-oriented and are are generally of use to UK lawyers only in international practice areas. Findlaw also provides country-specific searching. However, for the UK lawyer this still suffers from its US provenance. There are no direct UK-based equivalents, so you are probably better off using a standard search engine or using one of the UK legal portals mentioned in the following section.

When using search engines to find legal materials on the web, bear in mind that you will only find what is publicly available. In the first place, don't expect to find the text of all current statutes or SIs on the web: they are just not there. At present **HMSO** publishes Acts from 1996 and SIs from 1997. Texts of some other Acts and SIs may well be available on other sites, but these will be non-official versions.

You will also not find *on* the web materials which may nevertheless be deliverable over it. Many text databases are stored off-line and the data is only 'served up' onto the web when a specific request is keyed in on the web search page by the user. Because the data itself is off- line, it cannot be indexed by the global search engines. Good examples are the judgment databases maintained by the **Court Service** and **Smith Bernal** (see p 55). There is free access to these databases, but only via the search page on each site.

Finally you will not find with a search engine web pages which are held in protected areas of a publisher's web server, for the same reason that the search engines don't have access.

Statute Law			
	Resources	*Update*	*Findit!*
UK Statutes	HMSO: Acts since 1/1/1996 *infolaw*: Acts alphabetically Acts chronologically	What's new on the HMSO site	Search the HMSO site
UK Statutory Instruments	HMSO: Statutory Instruments since 1/1/1997		
Devolved legislation	Scottish legislation Welsh legislation Northern Ireland legislation		
Bills	Parliament: Public Bills before UK Parliament	Progress on UK Bills	Search the UK Parliament site
Consultative Documents	The Stationery Office: Command Papers The Stationery Office: Other Consultative Documents	Stationery Office publications by date	
Parliamentary Proceedings	UK Parliament: House of Commons Publications	House of Commons: What's new House of Commons: Weekly information Bulletin	Search the UK Parliament site
	Parliament: House of Lords Publications		

Links to UK primary law sies and search engines are maintained on Nick's info-law: Lawfinder pages (pictured above).

Tell me more!

For the real enthusiast or aspiring search engine junkie there is a huge amount of information and statistics about search engines on the **Search Engine Watch** site at www.searchenginewatch.com.

Portals

Links to UK legal portal sites are at www.infolaw.co.uk/ifl/law.htm#Gateways

A portal (or gateway), as the word implies, is a site designed to provide access to the web. Portals are flavour of the month these days, as a successful site will attract a high volume of traffic which will in turn attract advertising revenue and other commercial opportunities. It is considered that each *registered* user of a (portal) site will generate in the region of £1,000 per annum. Hence the rush to attract users with free services.

But what defines a portal? how much use are they to lawyers? and are there any specifically designed for UK lawyers?

Global portals

All the well-known search engine sites have developed into portal sites. Recognising that most web users do not like just searching for things (or are not very good at it), these sites now provide classified indexes to their content. The first and most popular index of this type is that provided by **Yahoo**, though all the major search engines have followed suit. On most of these sites, being geared to the market at large, 'Legal Services' or some such categorisation will be buried a layer or two below the top level 'Business and Finance' classification. Although these sites index a very large number of web pages (but even the best manage only 15% or so), there may often be surprisingly few entries under a particular classification. Alternatively, if classifications are not specific enough, there may be too many entries for easy browsing. Nevertheless, despite these shortcomings, these indexes provide an alternative path into the web – and one which will often deliver results which would not readily be found with a word search.

Internet service providers have also generally developed their sites into portals. By their nature, they are the sites which many users initially access when logging on to the internet (whether by default or choice) and, rather than relying on revenue from subscription payments for their services, they are rapidly recognising the opportunities that their large user bases provide – developing business relationships and alliances with providers of other services which can all be accessed from the one entry point. But, while these sites may provide access to a wide range of services, within any one market sector the services will be limited to those provided by their business partners. So, for example, in the UK, the much-publicised Freeserve offers only a single (chargeable) service under its Legal Services heading.

UK legal portals

So what is available specifically for lawyers? The US **FindLaw** site is an example of the type of portal site described above designed specifically for the legal community, with a focused search engine, classified indexes and other facilities. It will, however, be of limited use to the UK lawyer apart from those areas of practice where the international dimension is of importance. While there is no direct equivalent in the UK, there are a number of sites providing useful indexes of legal resources for the UK lawyer. Two with the longest provenance are our own sites, which both present, in different ways, classified indexes of lawyers, legal resources and lawtech on the web. Another useful index is **Go Interactive**'s Access to Law on the Internet, also published on the **Society for Computers and Law** site. As well as UK law, this index covers Australian and New Zealand resources. For a more academic slant, two of the best indexes are those maintained by Sarah Carter for the Templeman Library at the **University of Kent at Canterbury** and the Law Links by Subject Area at the National Centre for Legal Education at **Warwick University**.

A number of providers have attempted to set up online legal communities. These differ from portal sites in that they seek to provide a one-stop-shop for the lawyer rather than facilitating access to the wide world beyond. In this category fall **Lawlink UK**, the UK version of the like-named Irish service established with some success at a time when there was little else available for Irish lawyers. Lawlink provides secure email and discounted access to services such as Extel company reports, RM Online company searches Dunn & Bradstreet company credit reports and Infolink legal and business news and reports. A more recent entrant is **Lawyers Online** which describes itself as a 'dedicated internet service provider for lawyers'. It provides free internet access and secure email, hosts discussion groups and is developing other content and services. (For those hoping for a quick look, note that there are no less than 25 graphics on the home page.) A more recent entrant is **legalISP.net**, published by Stat Plus.

Chapter 7

Purchasing Things on the Web

Contents

What's driving the development of the internet today is e-commerce – that is buying and selling goods and services electronically, specifically on the internet. E-commerce is not new – people have been using the internet to offer goods and services for sale and to obtain payment for them for several years. But there has been a huge cultural shift in recent years.

The internet is no longer the province of academics and techies; it is no longer simply a huge billboard blaring out the corporate message: it is a place where people with everyday needs can seek to have those fulfilled – most often successfully. We have, though, some way to go in the UK to overcome our natural conservatism and to perceive the internet as an opportunity rather than a threat. According to a recent survey, a majority of us believe it's a threat to morality, half that it encourages fraud, a third that it is a threat to security and nearly three quarters that it should be regulated. By contrast, more than three quarters of American internet users say it has improved their lives.

This chapter looks at e-commerce from the point of view of you, the buyer, with some examples of the sort of transactions most relevant to your everyday business. The following chapter looks at the web as a medium for marketing and selling *your* services.

Buying Goods

Suppliers have been working hard and fast to improve the internet 'buying experience' for you the consumer. Below are some examples of the success stories – services that will frequently be used in a business context. They are examples of services that will improve your life as a lawyer and business person. Even if you are sceptical of the value of current information and other resources on the web, these services alone offer a compelling reason for you to use the internet. (Anecdotal evidence suggests that the *most* compelling reason thirty- and forty-somethings find to use the web is helping the kids with their homework.)

Buying books

One of the biggest internet success stories of the late 90s has been the **Amazon** online book store, whose UK website is at www.amazon.co.uk. (That the substantial increase in its stock value is based more on the needs of the stock market than on earnings projections is another story.) Amazon has succeeded because it is has a huge catalogue of books it can supply at competitive – often heavily discounted – prices, and a very easy-to-use site, and because it offers an incredibly high level of service. You search its catalogue using authors' names and/or words in the title. Your hits are listed with bibliographic details and prices. You click to view fuller details and readers' reviews. Having decided to buy you click to add it to you shopping basket. You continue browsing and adding to your basket until you're done. Proceed to the checkout, select the shipping method, type in your details, including credit card number and send. Receive immediate email confirmation of your order, followed by confirmation of despatch and await delivery.

There is now intense competition in this market, with **Waterstones**, **WH Smith** and others entering the fray (and Amazon diversifying into other markets), and constant change is to be expected.

Buying law books

Hammicks
Legal Bookshops Online

Bookshop   News & Info   Contact Us

For further information or to Order, please click on your chosen title.
H = *Full Description Available*

Items 1 to 3 of 3
Using search: *chitty contracts*

H Chitty on contracts
    Edited by: Hugh Beale
    Publisher: Sweet & Maxwell **Publication date:** Oct 1999 **Binding:** Hardback
    Price: £ 265.00 **Edition:** 28th Ed
    Extract: Provides coverage of all aspects of contract law. This work is divided ...

H Chitty on contracts 2nd supplement
    Edited by: A.G. Guest, QC
    Publisher: Sweet & Maxwell **Publication date:** Dec 1997 **Binding:** Paperback
    Price: £ 40.00 **Edition:** 27th Ed
    Extract: This 1997 supplement brings "Chitty on Contracts" up to date.

Most of the law book publishers will offer you online ordering facilities from their websites, which are well and good if you know the book you want and its publisher. But far easier is to visit the online version of a law bookstore where the wares of all law book publishers can be found. The first such law book site geared to the UK market was **Law Books Online** at www.lawbooks-online.com, which maintains details of 18,000 (UK and overseas) law books in its catalogue. The shopping experience is not nearly as slick as with Amazon, but you can be reasonably sure of tracking down just about any law book you may require.

More recently **Hammicks** at www.hammickslegal.co.uk and **Blackwell Retail** at bookshop.blackwell.co.uk have entered the online market and **Waterlow** provide a Legal Bookfinder at waterlow.abasoft.co.uk.

A sample search for 'Chitty on Contracts' illustrates some of the differences between these sites (but should not necessarily be used to generalise about them).

- Blackwell provides a Quick Search by author or title or a Full Search using other criteria, including date and price range – the most detailed facility of the sites reviewed. The search produced eight hits. Although a number of these were out of print editions, these can be ordered as Blackwell provides an out of print book ordering facility through specialist search agents. The additional items in the list do, though, get in the way. The summary listing provides details of title, format, date and price and leads to full bibliographic details, though no extract.

- After clicking through an unnecessary opening screen, Hammicks provides a search by author, title, keywords or ISBN. The search produced three hits –

the last edition and supplement and the forthcoming edition. A full descriptions and a useful contents listing is provided. Hammicks also provide law book news and further information.

- With Law Books Online, again one needs to pass an unnecessary opening graphic, and then click on a not-immediately-apparent link to the search screen. Searching is by title, ISBN, subject or author. The search produced the same three hits as Hammicks but with no details at all on the summary screen other than title. There is a cursory summary and no edition date is given.

- Waterlows provides a search by subject, title, author or ISBN. The search produced two hits, both for the same 1994 edition. Full bibliograhic details are given. There is no ordering facility.

Buying a computer

Dell Computers has been a success story from the word go about 10 years ago, pioneering the concept of mail order computer sales. In 1998 its website at www.dell.co.uk was redesigned and now generates more than £1 million in orders per day. Although part of this success is down to the fact that Dell was successful beforehand, it has taken care to implement features which add value to your shopping trip and make online ordering far quicker than any other method.

Firstly, by asking a couple of simple questions about you and your needs, the Dell site quickly directs you to the type of system most suited to your profile. Second, having displayed details of a standard configuration and price for the selected model, it allows you to view and select alternative component specifications and optional extras such as printers, with each change recalculating the price. If human assistance is required, you can simply click on 'phone me', tap in your phone number and await a call-back within minutes.

Using a site such as this can probably cut down the elapsed time taken to select and order a new PC from perhaps days to a matter of minutes. Also, as specifications and prices change frequently, you're better off checking the latest offerings on the web, rather than looking at that brochure you received last month. (One of us was recently told that a brochure received that day was out of date!)

Other leading computer suppliers such as **Gateway** at www.gateway.com and **Compaq** at www.compaq.co.uk have followed Dell's lead and now operate similar sites.

Buying Software and Information

Software

Buying software is a doddle on the internet. The big plus here is that delivery is virtually instantaneous: there are no physical goods to ship, just digits down the wire. Of course, many will fear the risk of viruses, but anti-virus precautions need to be taken whatever you download from the web or save from your email.

On that subject, a purchase of Norton anti-virus softwarefrom **Symantec** at www.symantec.com is a good example of this type of transaction. From the Symantec site you can download a 30-day evaluation version – good enough to fix an immediate problem. For the next 30 days the installed program reminds you that your free ride is running out and, after 30 days, each day informs you it is no longer working. As intended, you soon gave in – 'Buy Now' you cry. Norton fires up your browser and connects you to the Symantec site. After tapping in your details and agreeing to part with about half the cost of the shrink-wrapped product in a high street store, the program automatically downloads a piece of code to unlock the evaluation version. All over in a few minutes and relatively painless.

A particular type of legal software which is readily available for purchase on the web is law forms – see p 59. Apart from this, the legal software suppliers do not generally sell their software over the web.

Information services

Most of this book is concerned with information services on the web that will assist the lawyer. The majority of the services described are free, though increasingly commercial publishers – including the new breed of smaller web publishers – have introduced chargeable 'premium' services, with free access limited to news areas, summaries or samples. Thus, for example:

- The principal law publishers (see Chapter 4) all offer their premium services on subscription. As well as providing information online, they may also offer ancillary services such as transcripts delivered in hard copy, by fax and/or electronically and an 'expert' helpline for answering legal questions.

- Companies such as **RM Online** offer company and trade mark searches.

Typically, the subscription services are charged by way of annual fee, and while this may be collected online from your credit card account, it may also be charged by invoice or to an existing account. Subscriptions can, of course, be set up for shorter periods, and there is at least one instance of a service which offers a day's subscription, enabling the casual or infrequent user to access the site without incurring a large charge.

Searches, software downloads and other services which can be monitored as individual transactions are generally charged per transaction, and if an account is set up, transactions may be charged monthly on an itemised bill.

Despite much talk, no examples of pay-per-view are known to be implemented amongst these publishers.

Chapter 8

Lawyers Doing Business on the Web

Contents

In the first edition of this book, which was written over the Summer of 1997, there was very little mention of lawyers doing actual business on the web. The firms and chambers with web pages were relatively few but, more importantly, they were still testing the water as to what could be done.

Whilst the majority of firms' and chambers' sites, even now, are still in the 'brochureware' phase of their development, there are a number of sites which are developing into serious marketing sites or even into the direct provision of legal services.

Marketing for Solicitors

Most lawyer websites are designed as a marketing presence for the firm's existing services, where the client, once attracted, would become a client in the traditional sense, rather than receiving advice directly over the web.

The main method of marketing is to provide information on the website which is of genuine use to potential clients so that, first of all, they are attracted to the site and make use of it and then, when more detailed or personal advice is required than can be provided in this way, the potential client naturally gravitates to the firm concerned.

Three examples are given on the pages which follow, two small firms and one very large one:

- a specialist licensing firm, Poppleston Allen, aiming for clients in the licensing trade;

- an immigration firm, Gherson & Co, aiming for overseas clients wishing to come to the UK; and

- an Irish firm, A & L Goodbody, aiming for substantial businesses interested in setting up subsidiaries in Ireland.

In each of the examples given, the firm has identified clearly the potential market and has then made every effort to provide information of interest to that market.

Broadly, the information provided by firms on their sites is designed for either private individuals or for commercial and business clients. A selection of each of these is maintained at, respectively, www.venables.co.uk/legal/individ.htm and www.venables.co.uk/legal/commerce.htm.

Another aspect of marketing, where the firm is aiming to promote itself as an expert in particular legal areas, is the provision of free email newsletters. These are described on p 70.

Poppleston Allen

www.popall.co.uk

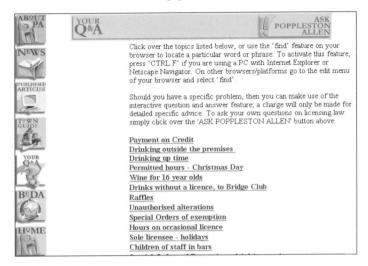

Part of the site is open to all visitors (in order to indicate the strength of the firm's knowledge and resources in this area) and part is open only to clients on a pass-worded basis (as a value-added service). The public areas of the site include news and articles and a question and answer forum, shown here.

Note that there is a section for the British Entertainment and Discotheque Association (second to last button on the left) for whom one of the partners is the legal director. This brings in additional visitors to the main site.

The client areas of the site provide something called 'Town Guide'. This includes the transfer session dates and full licensing policies for all the petty sessional divisions in England and Wales. The user chooses a town, and the database will produce the relevant dates and policy for the Petty Sessional Division in which the town is located. The user can then search through the policy for specific details.

Once the site was up and running, the firm issued press releases, advertised in the trade magazines, and told all their clients about the new services available to them. They have been particularly careful to ensure that the all staff know about the site and actively promote it themselves (not as obvious as it sounds).

Gherson & Co

www.gherson.com

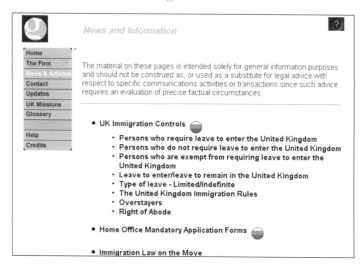

Gherson & Co is dedicated to immigration law including permit applications, business and investor visas, writers', artists' and composer visas, EU citizens wishing to work in the UK in a self employed capacity, and other aspects of EU community law in so far as they impact on UK immigration and nationality law.

The site is plainly aiming to be discovered in web searches; the meta tags at the beginning of the page include around 80 keywords, of which this section is just a small part:

> domicile, emigrate, emigration, UK emigration, persons not entitled to work in the UK, employer liability, identity cards, head teachers, hospital administrators, employment and benefit agencies, overseas nationals, discrimination, artist, writer, computer programmer, software writer, software analyst, computer analyst, composer, journalist

The site contains articles and summaries on many areas of immigration law, as can be seen in the picture. Another section of the site provides the address and contact details of all UK diplomatic missions around the world – quite a large resource in its own right.

There is even a choice of languages.

A & L Goodbody

www.algoodbody.ie

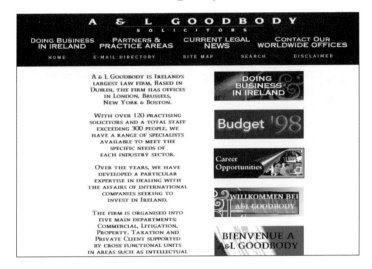

The site provides a major section on Doing Business in Ireland, with information on the geography, history and economy of Ireland, as well as the legal system, the regulatory system, taxation matters, and other areas. There is also a welcome in French and German!

In fact, several large firms in Ireland make a feature of Ireland as a business centre, and a number of Scottish firms do the same for Scotland.

Legal Transactions on the Web

What about lawyers actually carrying out the work on the web? This was one of the topics covered by Richard Susskind in his book *The Future of Law* where (in 1996) he predicted that many of the simpler types of work, or the provision of basic legal information, would be carried out on the web itself.

Of all the areas on the legal web, this area is moving perhaps the fastest, challenged only by the speed with which the legal publishers are putting material on the web. We look at several different approaches to the provision of High Street services, as follows:

- the Kaye Tesler method;
- the Rapidocs approach offered by Freeserve;
- the Fidler & Pepper method;
- the Rothera Dowson method.

After describing these individually, the advantages and disadvantages of each methods are described.

At the end of this section, there is also a description of the Linklaters' Blue Flag service. This is a different sort of approach entirely! It is also covered in Neil Cameron's article below.

For direct links to all the firms offering services of this sort, see www.venables.co.uk/legal/selling.htm.

Kaye Tesler & Co

www.kt.uklaw.net

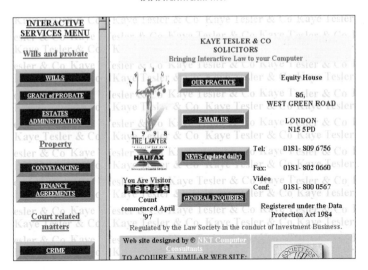

Kaye Tesler was one of the first law firms to offer services over the web. The types of work offered are forms-based; in other words, the client fills in the information on a form provided on the site, emails it to the firm, and the information thus provided is then merged into the appropriate documents, checked by the fee-earner concerned, and emailed back (or sent in the post) to the client.

The list in the left hand frame continues with Accident Claims, Contingency Fees, Liquidations, Directors Disqualification, Change of Name and Powers of Attorney. In each case, there is also a set of notes on the type of situation involved, including a clear statement as to the limits of the fixed fee condition, followed by a form where the client fills in the information required.

Michael Kaye contributes an article, 'Getting business from the Web', below.

Other firms who carry out work in a similar manner, ie the user fills out a form on the website and the firm carries out the work in its own time, include Briffa & Co, Kippax Beaumont Lewis, Eckersley Hope and Rogers & Norton.

The Desktop Lawyer

www.freeserve.net

The Desktop Lawyer is a service which enables legal documents to be generated automatically over the web, and is available from Freeserve, the Dixons free internet service which was launched in October 1998 and already has over 1 million subscribers.

Freeserve's plan is to capture many of the key home market opportunities in e-commerce; in other words to take a percentage of various mass market sales operations hosted on its pages. This is all part of the 'eyeballs' theory of the Internet – where there are eyeballs, there are marketing opportunities. The picture above shows part of the main screen from the Freeserve site (you do not have to be a Freeserve user to get the Freeserve site).

Imagine that you are an ordinary person with a legal problem and you click on the Legal Services button. You then see the main legal screen. There a number of categories of documents available. The Business section, for example, includes Acknowledgement of Debt, Agreement for the Supply of Goods, Confidentiality Agreement, Distribution Agreement and so on.

The process of actually getting the document is quite complicated and several stages are involved, including registering with the service, accepting some quite hefty disclaimers, downloading the Rapidocs Assembler software (this takes about 15 minutes online although Freeserve customers can take it from the CD they obtained when they registered), finalising the purchase, downloading the particular template file involved (like the will), entering credit card details (this uses the NetBanx system), downloading the small files which unlock the larger ones and then logging off. Once offline, you have to persuade your system to find all these files again and connect them in the right way and you then have to work through the document generating process, where the system asks you the questions and generates the document.

There are some very strong disclaimers in place, eg:

> We will not have any liability to you at all if you use any document without obtaining appropriate legal advice as to its suitability for your particular requirements. Whatever advice you receive is the responsibility of the solicitors or other person advising you and we cannot in any way be responsible for it. Nor will we have any responsibility at all for the alterations that may be made to the document after you have downloaded it or received it in any other way.

You can also purchase phone assistance, which then comes from lawyers employed by Desktop Lawyer, a company owned by Epoch Software, the originators of the system. Note that the questions are answered by lawyers but Epoch is not a firm of solicitors; there are interesting implications of this manner of providing legal advice which will doubtless occupy the minds of various parties in the months to come.

If more detailed advice is required than can be given over the phone, the system puts the user in contact with a member of the LawNet group, but at this point, the user becomes a normal client.

The Rapidocs software is originated by Epoch Software (www.epochsoftware.co.uk). Key directors are brothers Richard Cohen, partner in solicitors firm Landau & Cohen (www.landaucohen.co.uk) and Grahame Cohen. Epoch is a British company: there does not appear to be a US rival to this software at present.

The documents for this service have been drafted by 11 Stone Buildings.

Another company DirectLaw (www.directlaw.co.uk), also owned by Epoch Software, sells the e-commerce service to solicitors or other bodies who want to convert their documents in order to provide services of the same sort.

Fidler & Pepper

Fidler & Pepper at www.fidler.co.uk has been first with a number of new developments, including the provision of a facility for a client to see a status report on the Fidler & Pepper website.

In this latest innovation, the user carries out the process of generating the will actually online. The system uses around 50 will paragraphs to generate the will and the firm has applied for a patent for the process. Note that this is not a 'send me the information' operation; the user receives the document at the actual time of filling in the form (which could be in the middle of the night).

Rothera Dowson

Rothera Dowson, at www.rotheradowson.co.uk, in Nottingham, use a service provided by the East Midlands Shopping Centre. They offer legal products – wills, tenancy agreements, change of name deeds, powers of attorney and other documents.

Partner Anton Balkitis says:

> Unlike other websites offering legal services online, we do not expect the client to complete the documents themselves. The client gives EMSC their credit card and other details and we then contact the client and do the work. People may want to buy on line but not want to part with all their details for a form or deed. There is still a lot of concern about security. At least we can properly advise in this way.

Summary of advantages and disadvantages

With the Desktop Lawyer, the system can be expanded to provide many types of documents, with effectively a zero marginal cost. The disadvantage is that it is quite complicated to use. Also, the topic of liability and disclaimers is one which needs still to be resolved.

With Kaye Tesler & Co's method the firm keeps control of the work and will recognise when the work is not suitable for the method, but the operation cannot address a mass market.

Fidler & Pepper's approach is immediate and also a very nice system to use – the most pleasant, for the user, of any yet seen. The disadvantage is that each type of document has to be separately planned (legally) and then programmed, so that the number of documents available at any one time is bound to be limited. Also, if the law changes, the process of changing the document will again involve both the lawyer and the programmer. Again, this cannot really become a mass market.

One advantage of Rother Dowson's method is that the firm can become part of a locally based 'shopping area' and receive exposure to potential clients which it would not otherwise get. Another advantage is that the document or deed can be perfectly tailored to suit the client's needs as the client does not have to fill in complex online forms. However, it is really just an online price list and people may be unsure as to exactly what they are going to get for their money. However, the firm is offering their services at cheaper rates on the internet, in order to attract a new market.

Linklaters' Blue Flag

www.blueflag.com

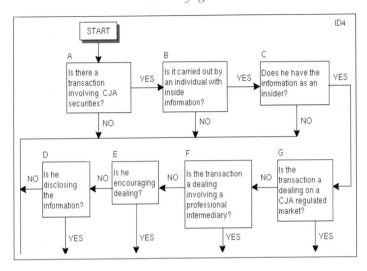

This followingdescription is taken from the site itself:

> Blue Flag delivers regulatory compliance advice directly to the desks of financial institutions via the Internet. It gives the legal advice they need when conducting financial services business in, into and out of the UK, Continental Europe and the Asia-Pacific region, regardless of where they are based.

> Blue Flag is for legal and compliance professionals working in investment banks, securities houses, commercial banks and fund management.

> Blue Flag is continually accessible on the Internet from anywhere in the world. It provides high grade legal advice on which the client can rely, backed by the legal capacity and experience of the Firm.

> It is structured as legal advice and, as such, goes beyond that which can be obtained cost-effectively from a 'live lawyer' for compliance purposes.

> Blue Flag provides the client with a rapid turnaround of advice. It has human support and advice available over the telephone. Its price provides clear value-for-money compared to the 'live lawyer' alternative.

Above is a section of a page concerning the criminal offence of insider dealing. The client works his way through the questions with explanatory notes provided at each stage and additional telephone support available if he should need it.

Getting Business from the Web – Practical Experience

by Michael D Kaye

When I started to study the internet, I noticed a tremendous difference between the way in which retailers use the net and professionals use the net. That difference has continued to widen and grow.

In the simplest of terms, retailers see the internet as an extension to their shop window, where not only can they display their goods, but they can actual conduct business, selling goods directly. Not a day passes in which there is not some expression of the growth in e-commerce.

Professionals generally and solicitors in particular, have not seen the internet as a similar opportunity. Despite the general belief that within a few years every solicitors' practice must have a web presence, relatively few solicitors have yet done so. Of those who have a website, they have designed an internet equivalent of a practice brochure.

The public perception of the law is that it is boring. Unless the public specifically needs the services of a solicitor, then they are unlikely to look at any solicitor's website. This is advantageous in marketing terms. The visitors who visit a website therefore, are unlikely to have stumbled across it, but are actively seeking a lawyer to represent them. A brochure style website therefore may well serve their needs. They will need to identify a solicitor undertaking the type of work that they require and who is conveniently located. Accordingly, it is right that every solicitors' website gives the potential client sufficient information to enable that client to see whether or not the firm in practice carries out the type of work that is required.

However, solicitors who generally charge in units of their time, fail to appreciate that, in their clients' eyes, it is not the solicitors' time that is of the greatest importance, but their own time, and there are a large range of solicitors' services that can be supplied, if the right questions are asked, and those in turn may be asked via questionnaires on the internet. Accordingly, it follows that those services can be dealt with on a totally electronic basis.

Various problems arise when offering services in this way, all of which are capable of being overcome with a well thought out and designed internet site. Areas that have to be covered are:

- sufficient disclaimers;
- client care;
- confidentiality (using a secure server); and
- payment (once again using a secure server for credit card payments).

Accordingly, whilst many important services can be provided to a large percentage of the population via the internet (wills, probate, conveyancing), there is an even greater rate of services which cannot be sold 'over the counter'.

The internet and email still can play a very important role in this area. Starting as an initial point of contact, a new range of clients can be found who not only seek legal services, but who are anxious to play with their computer toys. The experience of Kaye Tesler & Co on receiving conveyancing instructions has been that, not only do clients type up their own information to be incorporated into a database (saving input within the office), but they positively complain if communication with them thereafter is by 'snail mail' – ie the post.

The Kaye Tesler & Co website has been active since March 1997. The volume of work that has been generated has slowly increased, so that now hardly a day passes when there is not some type of communication via the website. Probably as high as 50% of these are communications which do not turn into valid instructions. What has however been surprising is the range of instructions that arise.

The conveyancing pages were initially designed to attract conveyancing work from around the country. Surprisingly, only a small percentage of the conveyancing instructions received have come from places which are geographically remote. However, the number of users of the internet has grown almost immeasurably in the last two years and continues to grow. The internet web page appears to act rather like an advertisement in a local newspaper, so that the majority of conveyancing remains relatively local to the office, but appears to have been attracted to our office by the website.

Even more surprising is that there is a class of users of the internet conveyancing website that had not been anticipated. Local estate agents, concluding a transaction, frequently on a Saturday afternoon when the offices are closed, will, with their client still in the estate agents' office, visit the Kaye Tesler & Co website and complete the instructions forms then and there. The website automatically accepts and acknowledges those instructions. The estate agent appears very efficient to his client whilst at the same time saving himself the trouble of sending out the usual opening letters on the following Monday. Everyone's happy.

A fact that is very hard for us all to grasp is the global nature of the internet. It makes absolutely no difference, in practical terms, if your potential client is in Australia or next door. Communication via the internet is just as quick. Those of us who live in the UK forget the enormous number of expats outside the UK. Frequently, problems arise with which they must deal. Further, there are many UK citizens working abroad, who have let their homes in the UK. A vast number arose during the period of negative equity. Accordingly, a well designed website showing both the ability and willingness to conduct work interactively, leads not only to instruction via the questionnaires on the particular services offered, but a wide range of emails from expats.

This second range of work from abroad, of course is not limited to expats. Indeed, the very first instruction that Kaye Tesler & Co received via the internet was an email from a gentleman living in Washington DC, whose father, not a UK subject, held a large number of shares in a British company and he needed assistance in obtaining probate.

The Kaye Tesler & Co website was designed to attract work of certain types, to be dealt with interactively. While it has attracted such work, it is right to say that it has also attracted a large volume of enquiries which are valueless. This is the equivalent of a high street practice having people just walk in the door with enquiries. In order to save time, a polite letter has been drafted into a word-processed file, and that letter is sent as an attachment to an email response to those enquiries. It is now considered that, dealing with such an enquiry now takes no longer than two to three minutes of office time.

There has been a noticeable increase in the flow of instructions over the two year period, and it is believed that the flow of instructions will increase even more, especially in a year or so when internet services will become available via digital television. There can be no doubt that an enthusiast within an office can make or break the success of a solicitors' website, but there can equally be no doubt that the value of instructions received over the course of a year will pay for the website.

Kaye Tesler & Co have established their own company offering other firms the creation of a website with a news page, a brochure element and up to ten interactive services. All this can be acquired and leased at less than £200.00 per month, ie one probate case per month effectively means that the website pays for itself.

And the future? The Government's consultation paper, Civil.Justice makes it quite clear that the Government sees the internet as one of the major methods by which the public will access law in the future.

Michael Kaye was the first solicitor to offer legal services from a firm's website. He has written and lectured widely on the internet and also on other topics, including voice recognition and video-conferencing. He can be contacted on kt@uklaw.net or at Kaye Tesler & Co, on 020 8809 6756.

Legal e-commerce

by Neil Cameron

Legal services

Sometimes known as 'productisation' or 'commoditisation', the idea of being able to encapsulate, or package, legal particular types of services as products is fairly recent and not entirely accepted.

However, in the same way as financial services institutions now talk about financial 'products', it is possible to contemplate a similar approach to some, by no means all, legal services.

The first examples were $40, or in the UK £40, wills which were generated via an online form on the internet. One of the first UK firms to adopt such a process, Kaye Tesler & Co, now offer similarly automated services for change of name and powers of attorney, as well as online forms for instructions for a range of matters including conveyancing, unfair dismissal, estates administration, matrimonial and others.

Nevertheless, most large firms did not take such developments seriously; an oft repeated mantra was, 'our work is very high value and low volume; and as it is not routine or predictable, it is not amenable to the application of automated techniques'.

I never believed that this applied across the board in relation to case management in large firms, and I do not believe it applies to online services provision either.

In any event, Linklaters blew a hole in this argument once and for all when they launched their internet-based Blue Flag service over two years ago.

The more prescient competitors were amazed, astonished and galvanised into action – Clifford Chance launched their own NextLaw service in 1999.

The less prescient still think that Linklaters are bringing the profession into disrepute, that all the Blue Flag users are mad and if they close their eyes long enough the whole problem will go away.

Well, it won't – as Richard Millhouse Nixon once stated, 'you can't put the toothpaste back in the tube'.

Blue Flag and NextLaw have shown that online 'productisation' can be applied to high value legal services, and Kaye Tesler & Co have shown that it can be exploited by high street practices.

What do they do?

I have not had a chance to see NextLaw, but Blue Flag provides extensive up to date information regarding the various primary, secondary and tertiary regulations that apply to the sale and supply of financial instruments throughout the jurisdictions of the European Union. If you look up a topic in relation to, say, France, then you can jump sideways to the same rules that would apply to the same activity in any other EU country.

It even advises on inter-jurisdictional issues; for example, if you look up the rules for cold-calling to sell insurance in, say, Spain – it is not only capable of telling you whether a call can be made within Spain, but from any other EU country to Spain, and vice versa.

Blue Flag UK is more extensive and has flow-charts with built-in automated logic. So, for example, if you want to know whether a person is guilty of insider dealing, you can follow the flow-chart through answering each Yes/No question (having regard to the explanatory notes and definitions that are available via hypertext links) and lead through to the conclusion. The history of your Q&A is then displayed in another browser frame for easy reference and editing.

There is now a Blue Flag Asia, and Blue Flag Funds – which is directed at providing advisory services to investment funds managers. One can only speculate on the next generation of Blue Flag 'products' will do; but there is good reason to suppose that it will include the ability to generate draft documents according to artificial intelligence reasoning.

In a related e-commerce move Linklaters and the document management system vendor Documentum (who provide the technology behind the content management for Blue Flag) have jointly launched a CD-ROM service called 'Blue Flag Confirms' which uses Linklaters know-how and Documentum technology to build very complex documents for sophisticated derivatives transactions.

This service happens not to be delivered, at present, via the internet, but it is still an example, and a leading edge example, of commoditisation and e-commerce.

Nextlaw offers information and advice regarding a range of data protection issues.

What can be 'commoditised'?

Not all legal services are suitable for this 'commoditisiation' process. It is likely to happen to the more low-value, high volume work, in which case the rates available for such work will fall.

However, that still leaves the higher value 'follow-on' work which should increase in relative value and for which it should be possible to charge a premium.

It is likely that the work that is capable of being commoditised *will* be commoditised. It is then likely that more and more law firms will enter this arena and that there will be a bloody price war. At this point, some law firms will start to give such services away for free.

If this sounds unlikely, just consider the example of Internet Service Providers over the last nine months. It was an established business for a range of prices between £8 and £20 per month. One supplier upsets the apple-cart by offering a free service, on the basis that the kick-back from BT and the opportunities for selling on goods and services make is economical to do so. Suddenly we have dozens of vendors offering free internet access. It becomes difficult to sustain a fee-paying service unless there is perceived added value.

It will happen this way with law firms – a firm which provides a range of commoditisable and non-commoditisable services will realise that it is in their interests to give away the commoditised services on the basis they will obtain the higher-value added and high cost follow on work. They will be able to do this as they will, by then, have recovered their investment in the automated services.

Others law firms operating in the same sector will be forced to follow suit. All hell will then break loose, and it is difficult to forecast with any accuracy what will happen then, but the existing model of charging and delivery of such services will be changed forever, and some firms will come off very badly in the process.

High-volume: low-value

There are increasing numbers of examples of high street type services being delivered via the Internet. For some time, there have been a plethora of US firms offering $40 wills, and we have since seen the £40 will in this country from Kaye Tesler and others. There are also high street firms with sites offering a range of other services, such as domestic conveyancing, divorce, change of name by deed poll, powers of atttorney, etc.

Dixon's Freeserve Internet service has gone one stage further, and the 'Desktop Lawyer' on their website offers a wide range of documents prepared automatically using the Rapidocs system, with follow up telephone support – some for as little as £10.

The competition

The really amazing thing is that there are not more examples out there from other top 20 practices – although there are many large firms with initiatives to do so. Some have already made announcements about future electronic products, such as Denton Hall and others, but few are delivering them. In a related move, Fox Williams has announced that it will be delivering document assembly via the internet.

Most of the putative large-firm initiatives are at the low-volume, high-value end of the scale. Hammond Suddards, on the other hand, has announced that it has invested £1m in developing a leading edge service at the other end of the scale, for domestic conveyancing. This service, HammondsDirect, will be delivered in association with mortgage lenders and apart from automating the conveyancing process, will deliver up-to-date progress information to the house purchaser and the lender, as well as to associated estate agents.

The second most amazing thing is that at a US conference last year, at a Web session by a large US legal technology consultancy, it became apparent that;

- they had never heard of Blue Flag;
- neither had any of the lawyers present,
- there are no US examples of high value legal Web services.

Although one large US firm has announced that it is buying technology with a view to developing e-commerce applications, no high-value internet-based services have yet been launched.

Thus, apart from financial services and data protection, the field is wide open and the opportunities are enormous, as are the potential rewards. Imagine the economics of a legal service that you perform once, with staff that could be located anywhere, and that you can sell many times over for almost no marginal cost.

It also means that you are building closer and closer electronic ties to clients and would-be clients for traditional legal services – and if you don't, someone else will.

Risks

So what are the risks associated with this topic? There are the standard commercial risks:

If you *do not* 'productise' those legal services that are amenable, then some other law firm(s) will, and you will be uncompetitive. Who can afford to offer debt colelction services nowadays without automation, for example?

If you *do* 'productise' services that are not amenable then at worst you may be open to professional negligence litigation, or at best you will have spent a lot of effort on developing something no-one wants to buy.

There are also three specific risks that run with legal e-commerce which must be addressed;

- delivering the wrong service;
- attracting the wrong client;
- providing the wrong advice.

The service

There are some ground-rules for the kind of topic you choose to provide over the internet:

- You can't compete with Linklaters or Clifford Chance on their chosen subjects on price, so don't bother.

- It must be something you know well.

- You should be able to perform added value work in that area, as that is where the jam will be – there is even an argument that the commodity stuff will end up being given away – certainly Linklaters could now afford to do that with Blue Flag if it made commercial sense as a lever to win higher-value follow on work.

- There must be a market for it, more specifically: regulatory materials; an area of fast moving law; multi-jurisdictional is good.

- Decide whether your service is directed at lawyers in the in-house legal department, or the client's end users – or both.

- It should be an area where there is plenty of opportunity for expensive mistakes for the client base – either in financial or PR terms.

Some of the services that you could provide are not immediately obvious – and they don't have to be 'legal'. For example, you could:

- have a service for high street shop staff on how to arrest a suspected shoplifter and what to do in specified circumstances;

- have a system that generated a contract of employment for an HR department;

- provide free services to clients such as access to: selected parts of your Intranet, their documents in your document management system, progress reports (see www.fidler.co.uk for an example in action), charging information between bills and to bills themselves.

I have been talking to law firm clients recently and be in no doubt, they want these services, and – again – if your firm doesn't provide them another will.

The client

If you have a closed subscription service such as Blue Flag you are in control of your e-commerce client base. If you provide access to services (advice or document assembly, for example) for direct payment then you need to take steps to ensure that only the right kind of clients, those for whom the service is directed, use it.

Otherwise, to use a trite example, Richard Branson may order a £40 will (perhaps, just for fun) and then die - leaving an estate managed by a wholly inadequate will, and a vast legacy of litigation.

The dangers here are so great that only a belts and braces approach will suffice, you will need to qualify *out* those potential users that are inappropriate, and qualify *in* those who are.

The best ways to do this will probably include a rule-based Q&A session as well as plenty of descriptive text, finished off, of course, by a wad of disclaimers.

I still foresee an eruption of professional negligence litigation against lawyers for delivering what would have been perfectly good advice, had it been delivered to the client.

However, that still leaves plenty of scope for delivering the wrong advice.

The advice

If you 'encapsulate' know-how in the old fashioned sense – a wad of tired and out-dated precedents – then at least a lawyer gets to correct known mistakes before they are used. If you 'encapsulate' know-how in an electronic service that clients use unfettered, then you could, to paraphrase the White Queen, commit six acts of professional negligence before breakfast; without even knowing it.

For this reason, firms will need to ensure that they have taken every conceivable step before making such materials directly available over the web. It is a truism that most know-how within law firms is not in a fit state to be delivered to clients, even for free. Many firms under-estimate the amount of work that will be required to make commoditised law of the requisite quality.

You can't do what firms do with internal know-how – put the least busy, least productive and least good fee-earners on it. It must be the opposite – only the best people should do it – and then the very best should quality assure it. Nothing less will suffice. Linklaters, for example, have stated that no-one less than eight years qualified did any work on Blue Flag. If a firm is not willing to contemplate this kind of investment in quality, then they should not venture into this area at all.

Nevertheless, many will. The risk of selling bad advice, or to inappropriate clients, remains high, and the profession as a whole, via the Solicitors Indemnity Fund, will end up paying for those mistakes. It could end up expensive.

However, do not be misled – the option is not to avoid selling electronic legal services over the Internet – if law firms do not do it, plenty of other organisations will.

The challenge is doing it properly.

Neil Cameron is a legal technology advisor to law firms. He can be contacted on 0973 165130, email ncameron@neilcameron.co.uk. The Neil Cameron Legal Technology Consultancy website is at www.neilcameron.co.uk.

Marketing for Barristers

The question has to be asked – what do barristers think they are doing on the internet?

For solicitors, it is fairly clear what they are doing; they are targeting particular groups of people or businesses for whom they would like to carry out legal work and they are also showing off in a discreet sort of way. For barristers, however, it is not quite so clear. Are they really expecting solicitors to surf the net looking for chambers with an expertise in, say, employment law? Whilst this may happen at some point in the future, we doubt whether many decisions as to whom to retain are in fact being taken in this way at present.

Of course, some chambers and individual barristers are 'there' because it is so exciting and because they are convinced that something will come of it – even if they are not quite sure what – but these are probably in a minority.

Most barristers setting up web pages probably have a rather longer game plan in mind: that of establishing a presence on the web so that, in due course, they too will be 'there' when it begins to matter. As already described in the chapter 'Who's on the Legal Web', most chambers are settling for a brochure type of website for the moment, and are probably waiting to see what else they can do with it, later.

As also described in that earlier section, a few chambers, and some individual barristers, are setting up sites with articles and case reports, and are thus becoming known as a centre of expertise.

One chambers with a strong marketing approach to their website is **2 Temple Gardens** at www.2templegardens.co.uk, who have turned a brochure site into one of the most significant sources of information on the Civil Procedure Rules on the web and have gained a great deal of publicity in the process.

Here is what QC Tim Lamb says about it:

> My task was to prepare Chambers for the changes in the Civil Procedures Rules and to exploit any marketing potential. A roadshow for solicitors seemed like a good idea but professional conference organisers wanted a financial commitment of £100,000.

> What about the Chambers website, a cheap and underutilised resource?

> Almost every member of Chambers, the staff and all the pupils, responded to the call – wrestling with pdf files; manning photocopiers; sharpening pencils; editing text; faxing, phoning, persuading, cajoling the website providers; folding flyers; stuffing envelopes, loading email address books.

Within 48 hours of the CPR appearing on the Lord Chancellor's site we had our commentary, one of the first, posted on the Internet. Following our first notice in the *Times* we had over 3,000 hits in one day.

The day our second notice appeared followed by a mention in the Times legal 'diary' – another 7,000 hits were made. We know that our text has been downloaded by city firms, universities, government departments, and high street solicitors …. In short by lawyers everywhere.

Now, litigation solicitors are contacting us to provide them with seminars and further information. We are responding with enthusiasm and plan to meet the growing demand as it arises. Teams of barristers from Chambers are now touring the country hosting seminars for existing clients and others who have asked us and to get involved with their legal training.

Cost – two small notices in the Times and some hard work from Chambers barristers. Rewards – the opportunity to put the name of this go-ahead Chambers in front of thousands of lawyers linked to the net.

In the Guest Article which follows, Tim gives his views on how barristers could use the web for marketing purposes and considers what the future holds for this type of activity.

Benefits for Barristers of a Good Website

by Tim Lamb QC and Charles Dougherty

2 Temple Gardens was one of the first sets of chambers to set up a website. It is right to say, however, that until recently it had not proved a particularly useful marketing tool. Prior to January 1999 what the visitor found there was a general description of the work of Chambers and a profile of each member. We did not display our website address prominently on our printed literature or at all in our advertisements. The result was that few solicitors knew of the website's existence and the number of visitors to the site was therefore very low.

In January 1999 Chambers decided to provide a commentary on the new Civil Procedure Rules. It quickly became apparent that the fastest, cheapest and most efficient way of disseminating the commentary was via our website. Within 48 hours of the Rules being published we had posted a 60 page commentary. We then set about letting the market know of our website and commentary by means of a mailshot and advertisements in the Times and the Lawyer.

Word spread quickly and our commentary obviously proved attractive to the legal profession, as we were soon receiving many hits, on some days, thousands of hits. The commentary drew the visitors in but from the site statistics we know that many stayed and explored the site finding out more about 2 Temple Gardens and its members.

The web commentary was only the first part of our plan to market ourselves as experts in the New Rules. Just as important were the conferences we held in the provinces and London. It is really at the conferences that potential Instructing Solicitors can see the individual members perform. If a member of 2 Temple Gardens fails to impress on the conference stage that is his or her fault - barristers should be impressive. No amount of exposure on our website can sustain a practice.

Our mistake until January 1999 had been to think of the website as an advertising tool rather than a marketing tool. A visitor is unlikely to stumble upon the site. Advertising is necessary to get people to visit for the first time. What led to the high number of hits to our site when we first posted our Woolf commentary was the advertising in the *Times* and the *Lawyer*, not the mere existence of the commentary on the web.

The following examples illustrate the effect of the broader marketing exercise, of which the website is is an important part. The day after our Civil Procedure conference at the Law Society (before an audience of 280) a partner in a City firm phoned up to book one of the junior speakers for a $400,000 arbitration, so impressed had the solicitor been with his performance. Further, our senior clerk has found the website a useful tool in bringing chambers alive on his marketing visits to the Far East.

Is the website cost effective? The site is helping to reduce costs. There is no marginal cost associated with each extra visitor. Handing out a brochure (containing less information) costs £3 a go. There is much to be said for persuading solicitors to visit the site rather than simply sending them a brochure.

More generally the website has raised our profile in recent months. It has helped cement our image as a forward looking chambers and it has opened other opportunities for promotion: we have received invitations to give dedicated talks to government departments, individual firms of solicitors and other professionals; to present educational videos; to contribute commentary for *The White Book*.

Maintaining a website is not easy. To keep a site up to date and interesting requires time and effort. Expectations of websites are increasing all the time. Gone are the days when simply having a website was special: the content is all important. A barrister's website will only succeed if there is a genuine commitment within the chambers to provide fresh content regularly. That can be difficult with a collection of self-employed individuals. In our case the publication of the CPR coincided with a strong desire within Chambers to present a corporate image. The CPR, of course, affect every civil practitioner.

What does the future hold? The clear lesson we have learnt is that in order to be a success a site has to be useful and interesting to the visitor. A website needs to be more than just an electronic brochure; ideally it should be a centre of expertise. We are currently looking at posting weekly or fortnightly legal updates within our areas of expertise. We are also exploring a number of other opportunities for the future including:

- Recruitment via the web. Processing hundreds of paper applications for mini-pupillage takes a lot of time One of the difficulties is that applicants often supply insufficient information. Providing a standard application form online would ensure that we had all the relevant information before deciding whether to offer a placement. Electronic storage of the information would help the analysis and sorting process and, hopefully, reduce the amount of paper the latter perhaps being a vain hope. It would also make the application process both easier and quicker for the applicant.

- Instructions via the Web. We are still a long way off from being able to deal with all new instructions via the web. Personal contact between marketing director, clerk and solicitor is important in building up a long term relationship. However, it may be appropriate to offer selected solicitors and other clients, insurers for example, the opportunity to instruct online for routine court or paper work.

The telex came and went. The photocopier brought an enormous change to civil litigation. We have only just begun to explore the effects of the net.

Timothy Lamb QC, at 2 Temple Gardens, is a common law and commercial silk and a committed convert to the internet. Charles Dougherty is a barrister at 2 Temple Gardens. A former management consultant, he has a particular interest in Y2K and IT related matters.

Contact: 2 Temple Gardens, Temple, London EC4Y 9AY; tel 020 75836041; email tlamb@2templegardens.co.uk and cdougherty@2templegardens.co.uk. website at www.2templegardens.co.uk.

Chapter 9

Intranets, Knowledge Management and Extranets

Contents

This chapter provides, first, a brief introduction to the concepts of intranets, knowledge management and extranets. The following section provides a case study – Mike Robinson and Heather Robinson describe the intranet installed at Bevan Ashford. They are respectively the IT Director and the Head of Information Services, indicating the close co-operation needed between these two disciplines.

Introduction

Intranets

An intranet is a set of information resources which looks and feels like the web but is limited to internal use within an organisation. It requires a modern network of PCs, running current versions of Novell or NT (which use internet protocols for moving information around the system) together with web server software to manage the overall information. The user then views the information using Internet Explorer or Netscape.

Typically, the information which firms provide on an Intranet is information which was previously circulated in printed form: telephone books, practice manuals, lists of experts and other rather boring information. This is a pity. The intranet really only comes to life when it starts to include sources of more interesting information, such as opinions and legal advice, information from the library, online information from the publishers, general web access (as covered in this book) or other data bases of interest.

Many of these more interesting resources are not initially provided in html format (the language in which pages of information are presented to the user) but require some kind of interface program to search the information source in question and return an html page to the person requiring it.

Knowledge management

This is really a natural development of an intranet. It means the management of a large number of different resources so that a single interface, and a single searching process, can access any of them.

Thus, a search made on a client's name, or a product, or a legal concept, could bring back information from the client database, the word processing archives including stored opinions and advice, spreadsheets, forms, email archives, the firm's diaries, the library catalogue (ideally the whole library online), external publishers and the many resources available over the internet.

To manage this information is enormously difficult not only for technical reasons (interfacing with different types of database and external resource is a major task) but also from the point of view of human comprehension. There is a real danger of vast quantities of information being dumped on the unfortunate user, without structure or any indication of its validity.

In some cases, the 'knowledge manager' is the firm's librarian, in others, a lawyer with special interest in information systems, and in yet other cases, an information scientist – effectively a separate discipline. There is a certain amount of jockying for position going an at the moment in this fast-developing field.

From the point of view of the system architecture necessary to support knowledge management, there are number of types of software available. The products themselves originate from different market applications, for example, **Soutron**'s 'Textbase' system (see www.soutron.com) has been developed from specialist library management systems.

Others come from document management origins, like **PC DOCS/Fulcrum** (see www.pcdocs.com), which provides document management and knowledge management software used by many large firms in the UK and the USA.

Other software available for creating and/or searching large knowledge bases comes from Cambridge-based **Autonomy** (www.autonomy.com). This is the software used by Butterworths for its Legislation Direct service.

Coming from a different direction, the Lotus Domino Notes system (now part of IBM), which was originally designed as a means of sharing information within an organisation, is also often used as the basis of an intranet. This works best for information created by the organisation internally, however, and is not really designed for accessing external data bases or different sources generally.

Extranets

Once you have an intranet, with a wide range of useful information sources available to you, you may wish to allow other people to share in it – it then becomes an 'extranet'.

In particular, you may wish to include your clients in the network. In other words, your clients are able to dial in to your network and, subject to passwords and checking generally, to have access to certain areas of your system. They can follow the work being done for them by the firm or they can access databases of information and advice which are relevant to them.

Several suppliers are working on systems of this sort, including Solicitec (who have won several awards for their product), Axxia, AIM, Select and TFB. Others will doubtless also follow, since this is one area of real interest and growth in the market at present. This topic is covered further in Chapter 8, 'Lawyers Doing Business on the Web'.

The access itself can be managed in a number of different ways. It can use a direct dialling facility to your system or the access can be set up using the resources of the internet as a whole (the public internet), with client access being controlled by passwords. If confidentiality is of even greater importance than this allows, then special software and often hardware can be used, with the network then being generally known as a Virtual Private Network, but this approach does not seem to have become established in the legal market yet.

The Intranet at Bevan Ashford

by Mike Robinson and Heather Robinson

An intranet is a private internal website that provides a common interface to a range of information resources including internal information and know-how, electronically published and online resources. The intranet is written in html and uses browsers such as Netscape or Microsoft Explorer, so that it has the same look and functionality as the internet.

Two years ago Bevan Ashford Solicitors began looking at ways to enhance our various databases and information sources. Our objective was to improve storage, manipulation and access to information within our network. We wanted to develop a flexible system that would continue to grow with the firm and would allow easy access to all staff in each of our offices and could also provide client access. The choice lay between implementing Lotus Notes or developing an intranet server. Bevan Ashford chose the intranet, because the technology is relatively easy and cheap to implement and the IT team were confident that they could support both development and expansion. The results have been extremely successful with our fee-earners, clients and staff.

Technical details

The firm has invested well in IT and has a powerful and reliable system based on a Novell network running Microsoft Office products. All staff have a networked Pentium PC on their desk or, for mobile users, a laptop and docking station.

We chose Microsoft Internet Explorer 4.0. as our browser and we are presently evaluating IE5. Using a web browser to access information provides one front end to access all information; it is also simple to use and requires little training. All PCs need to be running Windows 95 with at least 64mb Ram. Internet pages are generally very graphical and include a number of buttons or icons so it is advisable to provide larger monitors, at least 17".

The introduction of an intranet should not slow your system down as the software requires only a moderate amount of memory. For 300 users, the intranet would need to run on a reasonably powerful server, for example a Compaq 2500 with RAID 5, 256MB RAM running NT4 and IIS4 would be ideal for a Microsoft environment. A 27 Gb disk drive will give you scope to store the index for your search engine, should you choose to implement one. A simple system, without the search engine, could get away with as little as 5Mb.

We have a permanent leased line of 128K which provides our external connection to the internet. We keep the size of this connection under review, as more users are given access to the internet and more and more client communication is carried out via e-mail.

A Compaq server will cost you around £4,500 but there are cheaper options and you can even use a PC. If you also want to use the internet you can have a permanent 64k leased line to the Internet from £6,000 to £8,000 per annum.

You will also need an html editing package, for example MS FrontPage 98, MacroMedia DreamWeaver 2.0 or PageMill 3.0 which cost between £100 and £200 each. A graphics package is also useful, for example Adobe PhotoShop.

Search engine

A search engine is an important addition: the intranet will collect and integrate your information, but it must be accessible. Without a search engine it's like looking at a 5-volume loose leaf book without the index – you have all the information you need, but no idea of how to find it.

FrontPage comes with a basic search engine, or you can use MS Index Server, which is more powerful, but more difficult to set up. These engines do have limitations regarding the number of directories or external sources they can access. If you want a serious search engine you can look at Fulcrum which is part of the PC Docs/Fulcrum suite, Verity or Altavista, but all these come with a high price tag.

Expertise needed

Intranet technology is relatively easy to implement and there are a number of software packages available to help the novice developer. FrontPage comes with wizards and 'themes' to help you get started. For the more adventurous you can create your own intranet pages using FrontPage as your editor, but developing your own themes. With Adobe PaintShop Pro you can create buttons and images.

You may want to scan in your company logo, and for the more advanced there is Java Script which can be used to add animation, such as roll-over buttons, which move or change shape or colour. To get the best out of the look and feel and to link it to all your sources of data you do need competent IT staff or a good consultant. You will need someone with foresight and the time, resources and skills to develop an intranet.

Security and monitoring

To protect against malicious attacks we have chosen to implement Novell's BorderManager software, which not only forms part of our firewall, but it also acts as a proxy cache. The proxy cache enables us to store frequently accessed web pages locally, so reducing the access times to users. BorderManager has proven to be much more powerful and efficient than any previous proxy servers we have looked at. We can also restrict individual user, or group, access to certain protocols or sites. Novell's BorderManager is integrated into our Novell's NDS.

We also had to consider our internal protocols: security is always necessary in a shared system, but exclusion should be minimal. Allowing for levels of access to certain areas, from 'read only' to 'author', should avoid the danger of over writing or corrupting important documents. With care, sensitive information can be restricted to those who need it with password protection, and external access can be limited by a correctly configured firewall system.

At Bevan Ashford all users can access the internet from their PC. We can also see and monitor where users go: we need to know which pages are used and which are not. If a page is not being used, it may mean that the information is not relevant or – quite a different reason – that people do not know it is there.

If sites on the internet are proving popular we can make an addition to our Bevan Ashford favorites page, which contains links to legal, technical and Government sites as well as sport, weather and local interest sites that are of universal interest. Because users know we can see where they go, visits to 'dodgy' sites are minimised.

Keeping the information up to date

A major management problem for any firm is keeping such a system up to date. At Bevan Ashford, we have delegated the responsibility to the relevant support and legal departments. One or two members of each group have editing rights which enable them to add, amend or delete documents from within their group area and to create or break hypertext links to related sites. Meaningful key terms, headings and templates used on internal databases make this process easier and improves consistency.

- The Library manages the advice and opinions, legal resources on CDs, internet links, library catalogue and legal bulletins.

- Marketing look after our public website and maintain an internal bulletin board and the marketing calendar. In addition they update the list of press releases, proposals and tenders.

- The Accounts' section of the intranet includes advice and guidance on using our online time recording, and generally deals with accounts procedures. This section also allows partners secure access to view up to date management reports direct from the Unix accounts system.

- The Human Resources Department maintains a searchable telephone list, the office manual, a who's who and our Investor's In People policy paperwork.

- The IT Department's section includes information on internal training courses, question and answer databases, the network schematics and plans, disaster recovery policy, year 2000 strategy, and the fault logging system. There is also information about the servers, domains, Novell Directory Services (NDS) and other technical specifications.

- Each legal practice area has its own home page and distinct collection of materials. The contents of these are decided by the teams involved. Pages common to all fee earning areas include the Client Care index, team favourites (which are internet links of particular relevance) and an index of precedents.

Potential problems

Anyone setting out to create an intranet needs to be aware of some of the potential problems which will affect the system. It is important to understand the various licensing agreements that affect the holding of digital information. For example, we must be careful not to sell external or published information without the permission of the copyright holder.

In order to prevent unauthorised access, most publishers encrypt their data. This is a particular problem with CD-ROMs, most of which cannot be accessed directly through the Intranet, although there are software solutions available.

As part of the firm's risk management strategy, it is essential that active steps be taken to manage the currency and reliability of the information held. If users are to have confidence in the system it is important to decide a policy for identifying useful material as too much data will choke up and undermine the system.

The specification of the equipment available should also be considered and the system will need to be operational on the lowest and slowest PC. There are a host of security issues to consider in such an open system.

The intranet demands a heavy investment in staff time, which is expensive and this must be set off against any benefits. It is also important to timetable effectively and to be realistic in estimating the time involved in development – including interruptions and cancelled meetings.

While these pitfalls can create headaches for the IT department, the overall success of the intranet lies in the fact that those who utilize it are able to do so easily and that they have access to information that was previously unavailable to them. The successful businesses in the next millennium will need to be able to do business over the web and a comprehensive Intranet is a key part of such a process.

How does knowledge management fit into all this?

The aims of knowledge management are to draw together and then disseminate a diverse collection of information sources. Knowledge management looks to integrate internal, external and published materials and make it available in the most convenient format. The intranet comes into its own in this process as it provides a uniform interface to a number of different resources.

The introduction of a well structured and user friendly system is key to the success of a knowledge management initiative. Our intranet is organised to allow individuals to work outwards from their own small collection of knowledge: from personal documents to the team home page and departmental databases, to the general knowledge relating to the firm and out to the internet.

Bevan Ashford's fee earning staff are responsible for driving many of the new initiatives. The intranet is already accepted as a normal and natural part of the working environment, just as the telephone and e-mail have been.

The future

We see the legal information and knowledge side of our intranet becoming increasingly important. It already contains advice and opinions, with images attached when necessary, which are searched by keywords. Fee earners have access to our library of CD-ROMs and other information services such as our Woolf page and the library's current awareness bulletins.

For fee earners there is the immense attraction that the intranet's various internal and external databases can be searched through one common interface. Some Clients are already able to access selected information through our intranet and we see real potential for expanding this facility.

Michael Robinson is Head of IT at Bevan Ashford. Over the past five years he has implemented an entire IT infrastructure including a multi-location wide area network, email, internet and intranet, online information service and a paperless time recording system. Mike liaises closely with Bevan Ashford clients to facilitate improved communications and to advise on IT solutions.

Heather Robinson is Head of Information Services at Bevan Ashford, with particular responsibility for the development of the firm's knowledge management strategy. She has spent 10 years in the legal information arena and is the author of a number of articles on the use of the intranet as a knowledge management tool.

Contact Mike or Helen at Bevan Ashford Solicitors, 35 Colston Avenue, Bristol, BS1 4TT. Telephone 0117 9230 111, email m.robinson@bevanashford.co.uk or h.robinson@bevanashford.co.uk.

Chapter 10

Legal Education on the Web

Contents

Law Schools and Course Providers

Links to these educational sites are at www.venables.co.uk/legal/students.htm

- Aberdeen University Law Department
- Abertay Dundee School of Accountancy and Law
- Aberystwyth, Department of Law
- Anglia Polytechnic University Law School
- Aston Business School

- Belfast Law School
- Birkbeck College, Department of Law
- Birmingham, School of Law Home Page
- Bournemouth University, School of Finance and Law
- BPP Law School
- Brighton University, Department of Finance and Accountancy
- Bristol University Law Faculty
- Brunel University, Department of Law
- Buckingham School of Law

- Cambridge Law Faculty
- Cardiff Law School
- Central England University, Faculty of Law and Social Sciences
- Central Lancashire University, Department of Legal Studies

Cambridge University's law school listing

There are three very useful lists of UK Law School and College websites on the internet: **Butterworths**, **Cambridge University** (pictured above) and **Sweet & Maxwell**.

All Law Schools now have an internet component but the ones described below have made a particular feature of their internet access and/or have lobbied one of us for inclusion on our web pages. At least, that indicates an awareness of the power of the web and its influence on potential students!

The **College of Law** is the largest training body in the UK and has trained more than half of all UK solicitors. They provide a nationwide coverage, with full-time courses available at four branches in Central London, Chester, Guildford and York.

BPP Law School, in Lincoln's Inn Fields, offers the Legal Practice Course, the Bar Vocational Course, the Postgraduate Diploma in Law (CPE), the Professional Skills Course, the Qualified Lawyers' Transfer Test and the Law Society Management Course.

Semple Piggot Rochez (SPR) was the first provider in the world to deliver a full law degree over the internet, complete with virtual tutorials, online transmission of course material, net radio broadcasts, an online conference forum and access to Butterworths and Lawtel. This course, for the University of London (External programme) LLB degree, began in September 1997. The company also runs the first Postgraduate Diploma in Law (CPE) conversion course for non law graduates to be supported fully on the internet in association with the Law Group at Middlesex University (and see also Michael Semple Piggot's article below).

University of Northumbria Legal Services Unit organises short courses for solicitors and arranges conferences covering all aspects of the legal profession. The Unit has recently expanded and now runs a full programme of courses in Leeds and Newcastle. The School of Law is also validated to run the Bar Vocational Courses.

The **Inns of Court Law School** has an annual intake of 750 full-time and up to 100 part-time students. It is affiliated to City University and also runs a series of continuing professional development courses, organises international conference events and works with overseas law schools (including links with Europe, Japan and the United States).

The **Institute of Legal Executives** (ILEX) and its associated body ILEX Tutorial College (ITC) is a major provider of legal education through a series of local colleges and also through distance learning, with courses designed to allow students to study while continuing in their full-time employment.

Delivering Legal Courses via the Web

by Michael Semple Piggot

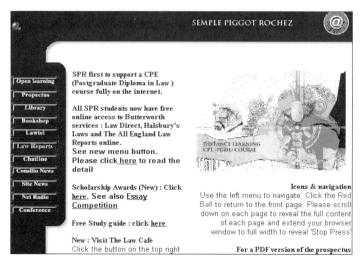

Semple Piggot Rochez (SPR) was the first provider in the world to deliver a full law degree over the internet (see www.spn-law.com). This course, for the University of London (External programme) LLB degree, began in September 1997. An online programme for the University of London (External Programme) LLM will follow in September 2000 and we are likely to be in a position to deliver an online MBA with a legal bias in collaboration with a UK University partner in 2001.

In addition, we run the first Postgraduate Diploma in Law (CPE) conversion course for non law graduates to be supported fully on the internet (see www.spr-law.com). We run this course with the Law Group at Middlesex University.

How the courses are delivered

It became apparent very quickly that if we were to deliver net based courses we had to design within the constraints of the net and student resources.

ISP selection was straightforward. We use Pipex and host all our sites with Corpex, who provide a high level of service seven days a week around the clock, obviating the need for us to maintain our own servers and technical support team. Office accommodation is minimal with a consequent saving in costs and administrative time. High level computer based administrative and accounting systems allow significant savings in staff costs.

The design of the site and the software technology was a far more complex issue. While we use readily available technologies (Acrobat Reader, Real Player and Java conferencing) the engine behind our delivery system was adapted for us by Telematica from their EASE system, used by the Open College and others, and tailored to our specific needs. We have now acquired a substantial shareholding in Telematica which will enable us to develop a very much more sophisticated internet delivery system over the next two years. All web design is done in-house and our team is fluent in all the leading multi-media authoring and imaging software packages. Within the next six months we will be moving to the use of Flash 3 and Shockwave and web database technology allowing us to bring in more multi-media material and generate web pages from a database on the fly.

The Law Degree course

We use a multi-media concept, where students select part or all of the online facilities on offer. All course materials (about 1,000 pages per subject) are delivered over the net (and on a CD-ROM issued separately) in pdf format. This allows students, no matter where they are based, to obtain immediate access online to course manuals, assignment and tutorial sheets and other paper based materials.

Increasingly, we are providing sound files (streamed and downloadable using Real Player and MPEG3) to provide students with lectures over the net.

Virtual tutorials are given in real time, scheduled to reflect different time zones, using a text based Java chat programme. Students log on from all over the world at a designated time and the tutor leads discussion on the problem question or discussion topic. The tutorials have proved to be remarkably successful and discussion has been as erudite and intelligent as anything I have seen in face to face tutorials with a group of good students. Full video conferencing will probably be incorporated within the next year to eighteen months, as the technology becomes cheaper and easier to use.

In the first year, to test our systems, we restricted entry to 15 students. Last year we restricted entry to 50 students (although we could have taken four times that number) and in the forthcoming year we will increase enrolment to a maximum of 200. The United States, Australia, Canada, Britain, Germany, Switzerland, Hong Kong, the Carribean region and, to a lesser extent, Malaysia, are our main geographical areas of recruitment. We even have two students from Beijing, China.

Our Virtual Workstation, powered by Telematica software, allows us to provide email facilities similar to Hotmail, discussion group rooms, bulletin boards and an entire electronic administrative infrastructure

Students are able to communicate freely with tutors (each of whom has their own subject page(s) on the website) and, more importantly, with each other in real time over the net. Students require a reasonably modern Pentium II based PC, 32–64mb of RAM, the ability to run version 4.0 or better of Netscape or Explorer, Adobe Acrobat Reader and Real Player plug-ins, speakers and a 56 k modem connection to the net. Our software does the rest.

All our students are provided with personal access to Lawtel as part of the fee. Students are also provided with online access to the All England Law Reports, Halsbury's Laws and Law Direct. Other electronic reference works and resources will follow shortly. The net is a fruitful source of very high quality legal information and the quality and range of provision of legal resources is certain to increase in the short to medium term. Our website contains one of the largest collections of links to resources on the net and we are in the early stages of developing our online legal magazine – Consilio – which will be freely available to all who visit the site. Presently, we give away 4,500 A4 pages of course materials for the benefit of students no matter where they are studying. We believe, strongly, that the net should maintain the ethos of access to free information and we will certainly continue to provide good quality material to students and practitioners as we develop our sites over the next few years.

Through LAWDIO, our video and recording firm, we have started commissioning 20–30 minute netradio programmes for broadcast over the net. We believe that interviews with practitioners, leading academics and members of the judiciary will enrich the student (and practitioner) experience and provide greater access to the views of experienced lawyers and commentators.

While we cannot replicate the experience of 'being at university' over the net (the great majority of our students are postgraduates in any event) we have been able to provide all the teaching elements of a university law course, including tutorials and feedback, online. Our fee for all the tuition is £800 + VAT per annum. (Students have to pay London University fees direct to the University.)

Postgraduate Diploma

For the Postgraduate Diploma in Law, CPE regulations require attendance at study weekends as part of the validation requirement. The website, however, provides a useful additional resource to students reading for the PGDL (CPE) on our Distance Learning course. SPR is accredited by the CPE Board to enrol 200 students and we anticipate taking a total of 160 students in September 1999.

Other UK legal education net initiatives

While most of the other net based legal education in the UK has taken the form of net based course materials published by individual university lecturers, there are few official university based courses on the net. The University of Huddersfield support their CPE course on the net and while there is interest in the development of net based courses in some universities (Oxford, Warwick and Leicester seem to be leading here) there is, to my knowledge, no full internet delivered law degree course offered by a UK University on the net.

In contrast, in the United States, Concord (Kaplan) and Regent University have both launched law degrees on the net. Other US universities are set to follow. There are over 10,000 education-based courses in the US in the final stages of readiness for delivery over the net. Britain is lagging behind.

We have made a substantial investment in net technology, the development of electronic learning material and, most recently, the acquisition of a major shareholding in an internet solutions and software house. We plan to continue with this investment strategy. The Scottish universities have already started to develop an internet plan. The English universities will need to act fairly quickly if they are to compete in the pool of global education.

Mike Semple Piggot, formerly co-founder and CEO of BPP Law School, is the founder of Semple Piggot Rochez, the legal training firm discussed in the article. Contact him on 020 7833 4306 or msp@spr-law.com

Semple Piggot Rochez's CPE courses are at www.spr-law.com, and LLB online is at www.spn-law.com.

Resources for Law Students

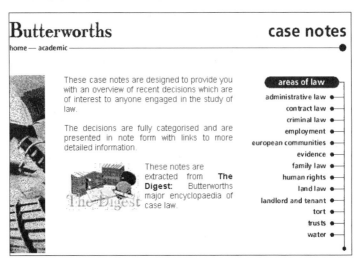

Student resources on the web are very varied and very good – and could well be of use not only to students but also to practitioners. Here is a selection of the resources available.

Butterworths provide a large selection of resources, including case notes, 'Law in context', links to Universities, and recreational resources.

Sweet & Maxwell offer a set of resources including 'Inter-Nutcases', which are various case digests of special interest to students.

The Student Law Centre provided by **Legalease**, offers very attractively presented resources, including legal news, legal updates, and careers information.

The **Incorporated Council of Law Reporting**, the non profit-making body which prepares The Law Reports and the Weekly Law Reports, offers a Student Newsletter with articles on law reporting and selected case summaries.

Bournemouth University School of Finance and Law offers a set of Subject Resources with links to sites, articles and briefings.

Semple Piggot Rochez, as well as providing full Law Degrees (see above) also offers 4,500 pages of course materials without charge. Most of the material is in pdf format – but you can download this program from the site.

MootingNet provides a structure and lots of background information for the old established occupation of 'mooting' (the play acting preparation for a legal career). There is also a useful set of links to other student resources.

Careers, Training Contracts and Pupillages

One of the main activities of law students is clearly trying to find a placement or job! There are several sites which assist students to do this.

The Student Law Centre, from **Legalease**, offers:

- A search facility that enables law students to find details of law firms offering training contracts and barristers chambers offering pupillages, using criteria such as region, work area and start year.

- Advice on preparing a curriculum vitae, interview techniques and timetables for qualifying as either a solicitor or barrister.

- A behind the scenes look at training at a range of different size law firms and barristers chambers.

The **Law Careers Advice Network**, as part of a site calledProspects Web, provides information on training contracts, mini-pupillages and vacation work.

Law Careers Net offers information on how to become a solicitor or a barrister, what training is needed, and also information on training contracts, vacation work, pupillages and mini-pupillages.

Chambers and Partners' Law Student Website provides extensive information on finding training contracts and the sort of firms to contact.

gti – UK & Irish Graduate careers provides a substantial section on pupillages and mini pupillages and general information on legal careers and placements.

For legal jobs online other than student-oriented openings, see p 75.

Organisations Providing Courses for CPD

Over recent years, the provision of CPD courses for the Law Society and the Bar Council (with the New Practitioner Programme) has become an industry in itself. For solicitors in particular, all of whom now have to attain their annual CPD points, there is a vast array of courses offered.

In addition to courses, the conferences offered by Butterworths Tolley, Centaur Conferences, EuroForum, Hawksmere, IBC, Nationwide and others all generally have a certain number of CPD hours available to participants. These are not described in this section but a selection of such events can generally be found at www.venables.co.uk/legal/conf.htm.

Here are a few of the organisations which particularly offer CPD courses and which advertise and support them on the web.

The **College of Law** offer CPD courses and in particular the very popular Legal Network Television (LNTV) which has provided high quality professional video training for tens of thousands of solicitors throughout the UK.

Norrie Professional Training is the first provider to be accredited by The Law Society to deliver CPD courses on the net.

Central Law Training is the largest provider of CPD training in the UK, offering about 3,500 events nationwide per year. Training is also provided for Paralegals, New York State Bar, Accreditation of Police Station Representatives, Post Qualification Certificates and Masters degrees.

The **Inns of Court Law School** offers CPD courses and other professional legal training programmes.

The **University of Oxford** CPD Centre offers information on Continuing Legal Education Courses.

The Centre for Professional Practice at the **University of Dundee**, offers courses including CPD, and makes extensive use of IT and the Internet in the course material.

BLS Professional Development deliver more than 1,000 public courses per year on all legal topics as well as law firm management. Most courses can be tailored to a firm's specific needs and delivered in-house.

Chapter 11

Scotland

Contents

*Links to Scottish sites are at www.venables.co.uk/legal/scotland.htm
links to Scottish firms' websites are at www.venables.co.uk/legal/firmscot.htm*

Scottish Legal Resources – Cyber Hame

by David Flint

For Scotland, 1999 was a momentous year. Now, for the first time in almost 300 years we have our own parliament, our own executive and our own law-making body.

Business Bulletin Minutes of Proceedings Written PQs	This section contains information produced by the Clerking Services directorate. It deals with the business of the Parliament, and records the decisions which Parliament reaches. **The Rules** These are the **Standing Orders** which govern how Parliament must conduct its business (external link) **Parliamentary Calendar**

Friday, 2 July	Last meeting before summer recess
Monday 30 August	Last day of summer recess
Wednesday 1 September	First meeting after recess
	2.30 Business Motion *followed by* Executive Business
	5.00 pm Decision Time *followed by* Members' Business
Thursday 2 September	9.30 am Executive Business
	2.30 pm Question Time
	3.00 pm Open Question Time *followed by, no later than 3.15 pm,* Executive Business
	5.00 pm Decision Time *followed by* Members' Business
Friday 8 October	Last day before autumn recess
Sunday 24 October	Last day of autumn recess
Tuesday 30 November	St Andrew's Day; no parliamentary business

The new **Scottish Parliament** is intending to put all of its material on line at www.scottish.parliament.uk simultaneously with its issue in paper form, but until the parliament is really up and running there is not a great deal to be seen.

Despite our excitement at the arrival of the Scottish Parliament, it has to be said that, for the Scottish cyber lawyer, the matter is largely irrelevant as much of cyber and e-commerce matters are reserved to the UK Parliament in Westminster.

The **Scottish Executive** site at www.scotland.gov.uk, explains the history and composition of the executive, as well as providing press releases and consultation papers. The work of each department is described, and contact details are given. The site is aimed at 'ordinary people' and it is easy to find your way around. There is also a most impressive list of links, covering Scottish Government and public bodies, Scottish Local Government, UK and European Sites, and other Scottish sites.

I regret that little primary material exists in relation to Scotland. Having said that, what Scots legal resources are available online?

The **Scottish Courts Website** at www.scotcourts.gov.uk provides information relating to all civil and criminal courts within Scotland, including the Court of Session, the High Court of Justiciary, the Sheriff Courts and a number of other courts, commissions and tribunals as well the District Courts.

The information includes location details, contact numbers, advice and details of recent significant judgments. Court of Session opinions from September 1998, including opinions in commercial cases from January 1998, are available.

It is not clear that all judgments are available. At the time of writing (June 1999), the Court of Session had some 270 cases reported for 1999, but only 17 Sheriff Court cases are on the site which seems less than satisfactory.

The **Law Society of Scotland** at www.lawscot.org.uk provides a list of all Scottish solicitors and firms and includes a searchable index of accredited specialists in various fields including Intellectual Property, Employment, Commercial Property and the like. This may be a starting point but, by its nature, is somewhat bland.

The main Scottish **Universities** all have law faculty homepages which purport to have Scots law materials, including:

- **Glasgow** at www.gla.ac.uk/Acad/Law/ provides no actual law.
- **Edinburgh** at www.law.ed.ac.uk/main.htm has a publications page which lists a number of books for sale but provides no useful primary legal material.
- **Strathclyde** at law-www-server.law.strath.ac.uk includes a search engine for caselaw.

The Scotsman newspaper at www.scotsman.com provides news, including legal news, but the Law Reports do not appear to be available.

For criminal law practitioners, a vast amount of material is available in the **Scottish Prison Service** site at www.sps.gov.uk which is well laid out and comprehensive. Equally the **Scottish Legal Aid Board** explains its procedures clearly and fully at www.slab.org.uk.

Even the police service has its own website at freespace.virgin.net/merlin.alba/ (there is a specifically Scottish section of this site) although my preference is for **Coppers Net** at www.coppers.net which is better laid out and doesn't have so many flashing lights!

Butterworths have a Scottish News site at www.butterworthsscotland.com/ scottishnewsdirect/index.htm, but, to date this is principally an advert for their forthcoming book series and offers little in the way of free information.

In relation to Scots law, possibly the area which is most technology friendly is the area of heritable (real) property. The **Land Register** at www.ros.gov.uk provides loads of information on the property system in Scotland. (It was the last Scots parliament in 1671 which established a uniform land registration system for all land in Scotland.) In due course the Land Register intends to have public search access (and perhaps more) on the internet.

The main **Solicitors Property Centres**, **Scotland** at www.sspc.co.uk, **Edinburgh** at www.espc.co.uk and **Glasgow** at www.gspc.co.uk all have comprehensive listings of available properties with over 10,000 properties on display at any time.

Similar services are offered by a number of Scottish solicitors firms – that of **South Forrest** in Inverness at www.southforrest.co.uk being among the first and most impressive. Whilst South Forrest have not yet achieved the whole conveyancing process online, the site shows what can be done with a little commitment and imagination.

In this article I have not dwelt on the information contained in the sites hosted by individual law firms. Many have comment pages on legal developments in Scotland, the UK and further afield. However, as far as I have been able to ascertain, none contains any case reports or uniquely Scottish primary materials.

On my own firm, **Macroberts**', website at www.macroberts.co.uk we cover developments in IP and IT fields and Construction and Employment. We do also have a large set of links to legal resources around the world.

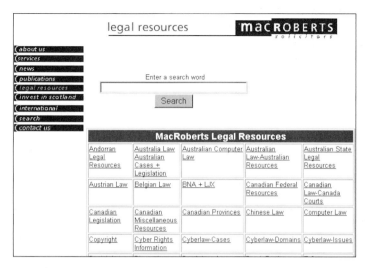

However, we have very little peculiarly Scottish material. I suspect most other sites have the same problem; whilst they/we would like to have more Scottish material, primary materials either do not exist, are not made available or are contractually tied to a single publisher (usually **W Green & Son** at www.wgreen.co.uk). The Greens site does have some case material but, unfortunately, the cases are of varying age (some almost 18 months ago) and are but a fraction of the cases heard or decided in Scotland.

In conclusion therefore, the position for Scots law on the Internet may be improving but it still far too early to throw away those books.

David Flint is a partner in Scottish law firm MacRoberts IP and Technology Law Group. He is a member of the Executive Council of the Internet Society Scotland Chapter and co-chair of the ABA International Business Law IP Sub-committee.

Contact David Flint at MacRoberts Solicitors, 152 Bath Street, Glasgow G2 4TB. Telephone +44 141–332 9988, email df@macroberts.co.uk.

Chapter 12

Ireland

Contents

*Links to Irish sites are at www.venables.co.uk/legal/ireland.htm and
links to Irish firms' websites are at www.venables.co.uk/legal/firmirel.htm*

Irish Legal Resources

by Kieron Wood

Traditionally, Irish lawyers have not been noted for being technophiles – but that is said to be changing. Ireland's Law Society Gazette claims that 'an ever increasing number of law firms are choosing to promote their practices through the Internet'. But, when one considers that there are more than five thousand practising solicitors and 1,200 practising barristers in Ireland, the design, scope and content of the Irish legal sites is disppointingly unimaginative.

The Irish Constitution	The Irish and Northern Irish Legal Systems and Courts	Irish and Northern Irish Government Information
Bunreacht na hÉireann Irish Constitution, Trinity College Dublin version	Summary of Constitution and Government of Ireland (from Dept. of Foreign Affairs)	Irish Government Web Server Government in Ireland (from Government Information Services)
Bunreacht na hÉireann Irish Constitution, Würzburg version	NEW: Full text of Irish Acts enacted 1922-1997 (from Attorney General's office)	The Oireachtas (the Dáil and the Seanad)
Divorce Referendum(1995) Bail Referendum (1996)	The Northern Irish Legal System	Members of the Government
Northern Ireland Agreement Referendum (1998)	The Irish Courts (including first official Irish Supreme Court judgment on the	Office of the Ombudsman (includes links to Annual Reports).
Amsterdam Treaty Referendum (1998)	web)	N Ireland Web Server
For historical reference:	Titles of Irish unreported judgments	N Ireland Information (British Embassy, Washington)
1922 Constitution (UCC)	1997-98 (from UCC law library)	

Legal Academics and Practitioners	The Peace Process	European Law
University College Dublin -	Northern Ireland Agreement Referendum 1998	Information about establishment of a Centralised European Convention Causebook
NUI Dublin	Independent Review of Parades and Marches	and Judgment Registry Database
UCD Division of Legal Medicine	(North Commission) Jan. 1997 (alternative site)	First full Irish legal publication on the Web:
Queen's University Belfast	International Body on Decommissioning	Full text of The Brussels Convention on
University College Cork -	(Mitchell Commission) Jan. 1996. (Click here	Jurisdiction and the Enforcement of Foreign
NUI Cork	for another version.)	Judgments: Papers and Precedents from the
NUI Galway	Framework Document on the future of	Conference held in Cork, September 1989
Trinity College Dublin	Northern Ireland, February 1995.	European Union

One of the best introductory sites is the **Irish Law Site**, provided by Darius Whelan at www.ucc.ie/ucc/depts/law/irishlaw, which provides a comprehensive overview of Irish legal websites. The site also includes the IrishLaw list, an e-mail discussion list on Irish and Northern Irish law with 350 members.

An impressive new site is that of the **Irish Law Society** at www.lawsociety.ie. This now includes useful articles from the *Law Society Gazette*, as well as professional information and details of how to become a solicitor. (See also p 29 for more on the Law Society site).

Claire O'Sullivan, webmaster of the Law Society site, says: 'We do have further plans to develop the website over the next few months by adding a members-only section, accessible by user name and password. This will contain access to the Law Society library catalogue, practice notes and directions and general information for solicitors. We also hope to include a bulletin board/discussion forum for members.'

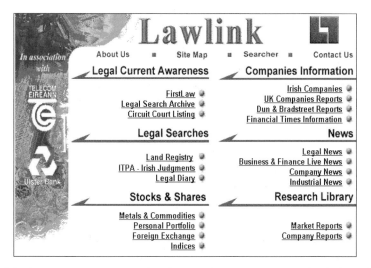

One of the longest-running Irish legal sites is **Lawlink** at www.lawlink.ie. A joint venture with the Irish Law Society since 1997, it provides a pay-as-you-go internet-based facility for barristers and solicitors. The site offers subscribers Lawlink (an online information system) and Securemail. Among the services offered are the legal diary, up-to-date judgments of the Superior Courts and law and company searches. The company claims to have signed up more than 400 firms with more than 1,500 subscribers, and 40 new firms being added each month. Lawlink also run a UK site.

The USA **FindLaw** site has a countries-specific section which includes an Irish page at www.findlaw.com/search/countries/ie.html. This enables a search to take place which will only return pages with 'ie' as the country code, and also contains a ready-made selection of links to articles and information about Ireland.

The **Legal Island** site at www.legal-island.com provides links to legal resources and Irish solicitors with either a web page or website – though at least one firm listed is no longer in practice. This site covers Northern Ireland as well as the Republic.

Some of the bigger firms have taken the trouble to put up more than just a blurb. The **William Fry** site at www.williamfry.ie features articles on banking and finance, directors' duties, company incorporation, employment issues, Y2K, examinership and Irish property law. Marketing Manager Paul Bale says 'the firm's plans for the site are quite fluid, as we like to update it on the run, rather than come up with a rigid, grand plan. Our site was completely overhauled a year ago, and in that time we've built it up into what we believe is one of the most information-rich legal sites in these islands. In fact, the tactic in Ireland seems to be centred on adding content, far more so than is the case in the UK generally.'

Ireland as a holding company regime

Opportunities for Apprentice Solicitors at MOP

Another wide ranging site is that of **Matheson Ormsby Prentice** at www.mop.ie. The MOP site includes copies of its Quarterly Comment publication, with useful articles on topics like the Freedom of Information Act, plus recent case law on issues such as charge cards, competition, pensions and product safety.

Aine Maguire of **A & L Goodbody**, Ireland's largest law firm, at www.algoodbody.ie says that, as part of the firm's new look site, the technology content had been considerably extended to reflect the concerns of major clients in the area. 'Our short to medium term objectives are to develop other specialist sub-site areas and to maintain these regularly so that they become a valuable resource to those working in the field,' she said. 'A large part of our site is dedicated towards inward investment clients who are thinking of setting up in Ireland. Overseas clients tell us they find this very useful and we intend to develop further in this area.' (See also p 139.)

The webmaster at **McCann FitzGerald**, solicitors, at www.mccann-fitzgerald.ie says he has received a very positive reaction to the firm's site. 'People seem to find the structure logical and simple to use, and they like the fact that there is plenty of material but no gimmicks. We are currently adding sections aimed at new markets (such as a recruitment section). We have had a large number of enquiries from potential clients directly through the site.'

Mason Hayes & Curran at www.mhc.ie intend to amend and update their new site in house every week, with legal news and recent transactions.

Only a few firms of solicitors seem to have registered .ie domain names, while smaller practices still rejoice in such memorable URLs as www.mayo-ireland.ie/Mayo/Towns/ClareM/WMcEllin/WMcEllin.htm

Smaller solicitors' firms in Ireland tend to use the net purely as a cheap advertising medium, without providing links or useful articles. The site of **Neil Twomey & Co** at www.iol.ie/bizpark/n/ntwomey is a good example of this – one dull homepage with a further dull page of services provided. And the **Kennedy Fitzgerald** site at www.iol.ie/~kennfitz is simply extraordinary. Just four photos and an address – not even e-mail! (The hopeful message 'to be filled in' – has been there for over a year.)

Frank Lanigan of **Frank Lanigan Malcomson & Law** at www.lowwwe.com/flml/ expresses the point of view of many of the smaller firms when he says his company put up 'a static site, in order to get a position on the net and to signify to our clients and other lawyers that we are net-conscious. We feel that it signifies our status as a technology conscious firm. We are using e-mail widely and have experienced considerable benefits in extra business and cost-reduction. We now insist on counsel e-mailing all documents to us, which saves a great deal of time and money.'

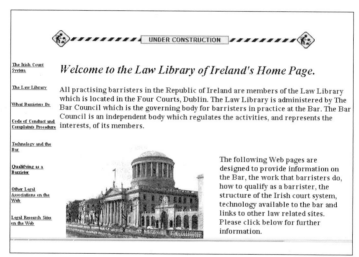

For information on barristers, the **Law Library of Ireland** has a website at indigo.ie/~gregk (so entitled, because the eponymous webmaster Greg K set it up!) The site features an 'under construction' banner, a black and white picture of the Four Courts and a meagre list of links in an eight-point typeface.

Webmaster Karl Lynch says he can't make any plans about the text content of the site but he does have some control over the design of the page in his role as webmaster. 'It's not a bad or ugly page, but there is room for improvement regarding its content. I receive a number of e-mails every week (mainly from barristers in the States) saying that they've found the site easy to browse through and high in content, so I guess the feedback is generally positive.'

(It doesn't include information about Irish barristers, but that's now obtainable through my own site – see below.)

Kieron Wood's pages

These pages contain articles, features and information on Irish legal matters

- Defamation Law in Ireland
- Want An Irish Divorce?
- The Divorce Act - Simplified
- Divorce Paperwork
- Family Law Statutes
- Where There's A Will...
- Legal Phrases Explained
- Legal Links
- Irish Barristers

Only one barrister currently has his own personal website – me, **Kieron Wood**, at welcome.to/barrister. I do try to maintain a considerable amount of information on the site. However, the history of the project has not been altogether smooth.

In 1997, the professional practices committee of the Bar Council of Ireland laid two complaints against me for 'touting'. Following a very full response to the complaint, the Bar Council has now set up a working party to establish guidelines for barristers' websites – and invited me to be a member!

Other Irish barristers are beginning to use the web too. Married couple **Denis Kelleher and Karen Murray** – experts on information technology law – provide information at www.ncirl.ie/itlaw/ hosted by the National College of Industrial Relations. The site covers areas such as copyright, computer crime, data protection, e-commerce, Y2K and what's new in IT law.

Fergus O'Rourke BL has information about uberrima fides, pensions and Irish insurance law at homepage.tinet/~ugf/

Barrister **Gillian Kelly** has a series of four papers on post-traumatic stress disorder as a recognizable psychiatric illness in the light of the 1995 Irish Supreme Court judgment in *Kelly v Hennessy* at www.telecoms.net/law/ptsd1.htm.

One brave barrister, **Twinkle Egan**, is attempting to set up a centralised European Convention causebook and judgment registry database at www.cyberia.ie/~twinkle.

Other sources of law in Ireland include government sites. But the **Department of Justice** website at www.irlgov.ie/justice/Courts/pagemaster_crt.htm is nothing short of a national embarrassment. The Department's Strategic Management Initiative document on Courts administration proclaims: 'Information technology is fundamental to supporting existing work and is also crucial in enabling change. Our objectives are to provide … maximum identification, and early delivery, of benefit from IT.' Yet the Courts Information page informs visitors: 'A dedicated Courts Information Website is currently being developed and in time these pages will be moved and hosted on the new site. There is no date yet as to when this might happen. Watch this space ….'

As of 3 August 1999, the site features one Supreme Court judgment from January 1998. (And don't bother following the link to 'Some sites and links of interest'. There are none!)

The webmaster promises: 'If you encounter any errors within these pages (ie links failing) please notify me and I will attempt to rectify the problems', but neither of the links at courtsinfo@justice.irlgov.ie or pagemaster@justice.irlgov.ie works.

But it's not all bad news. Irish statutes are now freely available online through the **Attorney General**'s site at www.irlgov.ie/ag. It offers information about the offices of the Attorney General, the parliamentary draftsman and the chief state solicitor, plus Acts of the Oireachtas (the Irish Parliament) from 1922–1997. Madelaine Dennison, law librarian in the AG's office, says the website has been generally very well received and she has received very positive feedback about the free availability of the Acts.

Oireachtas (Parliamentary) reports are also online now, albeit with 12–24 hour delays, and without Committee reports so far. The whole series of Dail (Lower House) Reports from 1922 to date is being put on CD, with a search engine. The second edition of the searchable CD of Irish Statutes, including Statutory Instruments is now available.

And the excellence of some Irish sites has been recognised by professionals in other countries. **Competition Online** at www.clubi.ie/competition/ compframesite/index.htm has just been named one of the world's top 50 legal research websites (and the only one managed from Europe). The award came from the US journal for law firm librarians, researchers and IT specialists, *Law Office Computing*. The free site provides links to worldwide competition, antitrust and regulatory sites – and features 500 searchable decisions of the Competition Authority of Ireland.

Kieron Wood is a barrister in general practice in Dublin. Formerly legal affairs correspondent of Ireland's national broadcasting service, RTE, he is also the author of A User's Guide to the High Court *(Four Courts Press) and co-author of* Divorce in Ireland *(O'Brien Press). He is a member of the Bar Council of Ireland's working party on websites for barristers. His own website is at welcome.to/barrister and his email address is barrister-at-law@bigfoot.com.*

Chapter 13

International Legal Resources

Contents

Europe

Links to European sites are at www.venables.co.uk/legal/europe.htm

News

Access to press releases from the EU institutions, the calendar of upcoming events, the official euro rates, the latest statistics and other news services.

Abc

Basic information on the European Union, citizens rights, key issues such as the euro and employment; access to official documents, legal texts, publications and databases, and sources of information

Institutions

General presentation and direct access to the home pages of the institutions: Parliament, Council, Commission, Court of Justice, Court of Auditors, Economic and Social

Policies

Access by subject to legal instruments in force, legislative activity in progress, implementation of common policies, EU grants and loans, statistics and

The starting place for information on the institutions of Europe has to be the **Europa** site. There is a vast amount of information here, most of it in eleven official languages.

The section on Legal Texts provides the full text of the treaties and legislation as well as links to case law.

Information on European governments (both EU and non-EU) is provided at Governments online, also a part of the Europa site. This provides a starting point for those wishing to locate and explore citizen-oriented information disseminated by governments and other official institutions of the EU countries (and also the non-EU countries).

The **European Parliament** site provides information on the history of the Parliament, the Members, the Agendas, Parliamentary Questions, Rules, References and Press Releases. The site also provides links to the National Parliaments.

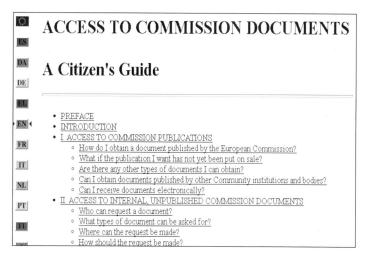

The **European Commission** provides press releases, work programmes, information on all the Commissioners, speeches of key figures and access to Commission documents. There is a Citizen's Guide which gives information on gaining access to commission documents, both published and unpublished, and information on decisions made. Note the choice of languages down the left hand side!

The **European Court of Justice** provides the full text of all its recent judgments. These can be browsed by period and there is also the ability to search for specific cases. There is a full index of cases lodged and a list of all press releases issued, some online.

The **European Court of Human Rights** also has judgments available and a searching facility.

The **International Court of Justice** at the Hague offers the text of the official judgments, advisory opinions, and orders. The decisions are published in English and French, the two official languages of the Court.

An index of European resources is offered by the **European Law School at Maastricht University**. There is a description of the legal system of each country and then, the particular links are grouped under Legislative, Judicial and Executive branches of the law.

For the individual European countries, we have provided a couple of good starting points for each country. Once you have identified these starting points, it should be possible to branch out into the particular resource that is required.

For example, a site called **Dutch Government and Politics** provides links to all the main legal and governmental resources in Holland.

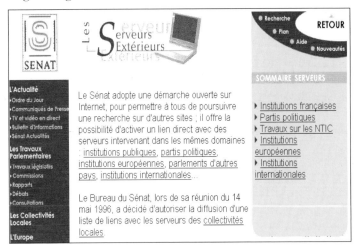

Most French resources are (most unreasonably) in French. The site of the **French Senat** provides history, parliamentary business and links to French legal resources.

German Law: Resources in English

(All materials in the links are in English, unless otherwise indicated.)

Courts and Court Reports / Statutes / Public Institutions / Miscellaneous Articles and Reviews / Lawyers in Germany / Other Links

(N.B. Information on Studying Law in Germany is also available on this server.)

Courts and Court Reports

- Abstracts of the Constitutional Court Reports - English summaries of the official press releases from the Constitutional Court (*BVerfG*) (SAARBRUCKEN)
- GLAW - detailed discussion in German of a wide range of Constitutional Court (*BVerfG*) cases, each with a brief English abstract (from Uni. Wuerzburg)
- German Law Archive - judgements, statutes and literature in English (from Uni. Oxford)

A major source of information on German Law and Legal Systems is provided by the Institute for Computer Science Law at the **University of Saarland, Saarbruecken**. The information is provided in English and covers Courts, Court Reports, Statutes, Public Institutions, Articles and Reports, Lawyers in Germany and general information on the Federal Government. Links are given to the full German text as appropriate. The University also provides a major register of information on European Laws and Legal Systems, with sections for each European country.

For Italy, a useful starting point is the **British-Italian Law Association**, which provides links to many Italian legal resources.

For Spain, **El Web Juridico** provides links to a wide variety of Spanish legal resources.

As to Irish legal resources, see Chapter 12.

USA

Links to USA sites are at www.venables.co.uk/legal/usa.htm

The USA is of interest not only because of its own legal resources but also because it is so important to the overall development of the internet itself. Not only was the internet invented there during the early years of the Cold War when the USA wanted a secure communications system, but it continued to be driven by both defence and academic research during the 70s and 80s and now, in the 90s and into the millennium, by commercial development.

All the big internet and IT-related companies are based in the USA – Microsoft, Sun, Compaq, Netscape, Yahoo, Excite, Amazon, Altavista, Oracle – the list goes on and on, covering computer hardware and components, software, and also the most advanced commercial exploitations of the new technology.

In addition, all the big legal battles seem to take place in the USA, such as that over censorship, pornography, encryption, privacy, free speech, domain-name management and ownership, taxation of e-commerce and competition policy.

From the rest-of-the-world perspective, therefore, the USA is of most interest as the harbinger of things to come, and the source of current commercial news.

FindLaw's Legal News provides a wide range of current legal news stories, grouped by major heading, eg White House Affairs, Microsoft Antitrust or Tobacco Litigation.

Here are some sources of USA legal news:

Law Journal Extra carries news about legal developments in the USA and provides links to other legal journals online and sources of news, including law technology product news.

Jurist: The Law Professors' Network provides breaking legal news.

West's Legal Directory provides current news items.

NewsLinx has daily internet news – everything you could want (and more).

American City Business Journals (there are about 40 of these) provides business and legal news.

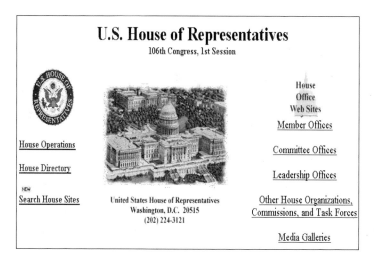

The **US House of Representatives** provides a major source of information, including:

- This Week on the House Floor: the schedule of bills, resolutions, and other legislative issues the House intends to consider this week;

- Up-to-date events on the House floor as they happen;

- The Library of Congress: information about the US Congress legislative process, bills, the Congressional Record, committee information, and historical documents;

- Today in Committee: information on committee meetings are updated hourly;

- Contacts: constituents may identify and/or contact their Representative.

The House of Representatives used to host a major resource called the Internet Law Library, but has now ceased to do this; the library has been taken over in various forms by other organisations.

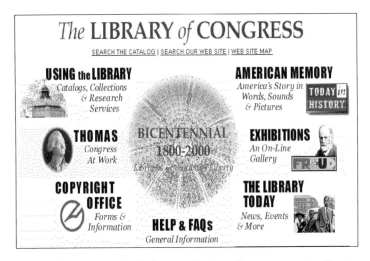

The **Library of Congress** site is designed primarily as a resource for the general public, with extensive exhibitions and links to multi-media tours of the past.

State law

- Alaska
- Alaska Supreme Court since 1991
- Alaska Supreme Court (recent)
- Alaska Court of Appeals, since1991
- Alaska Court of Appeals (recent slip)
- Alaska Court of Appeals (recent memoranda)
- Arizona
- Arizona Court of Appeals, Division Two, last 30 days
- Arizona Real Estate Law (once there choose "resources")
- Arkansas
- California Supreme Court decisions in MS Word & PDF format
- NEW California Supersite!
- California opinions (subscription only)
- California opinions (Findlaw)
- California codes
- Calif. Code Gopher
- California statutes
- California (Fully searchable case law and code database from 1934 service and a searchable database for Supreme Court cases. Free trial.
- Cal Penal Code - FTP

A major collection of State Law is maintained by researcher **Randy Singer**. He says:

> It would be very convenient if all state and federal codes, statutes, and case law were available on the Web. Unfortunately, economic realities dictate that we may never see all of the substantive law of all the states on the Web. Several states receive quite a bit of income by selling the exclusive rights to publish that state's case law. In addition, it is quite expensive to publish and maintain a

website, and money for such a project is not available in all states. Case law on the Web ideally would include decisions from at least the last 30 years, a sophisticated search engine for locating relevant law, case summaries, headnotes, etc. All of these are expensive to provide.

Given the above, it is impressive how much substantive law is already available on the Web. Most states now have a website with some substantive law posted but the quality and completeness varies considerably. Rarely will you see more than the last few years of a state's supreme court opinions on the Web. Often the opinions that you find will only be summaries. You will almost never see headnotes included. And though many sites allow you to search for a case by name, they often don't give you an index so that you know what cases are available.

University sites and law libraries

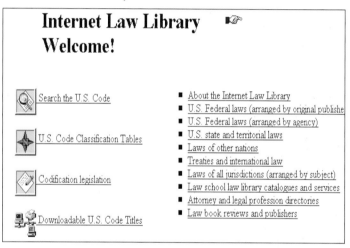

A comprehensive listing of legal sites and sources in the USA called the World Wide Web Virtual Library is provided at the **University of Indiana**. This provides lists of material organised by legal topic (Constitutional Law, Copyright …) and also by type or source (Treaty, Legislation …). It also contains an alphabetic list of Law Schools & Libraries and an alphabetic list of Law Firms on the WWW – with many hundreds of firms listed.

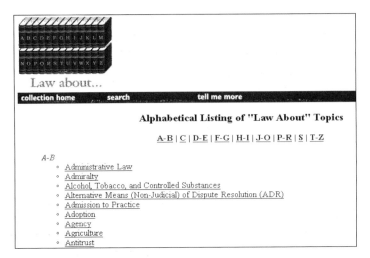

The Legal Information Institute at **Cornell University** offers the Institute's collection of recent and historic Supreme Court decisions, its hypertext versions of the full US Code, US Constitution, Federal Rules of Evidence and Civil Procedure, recent opinions of the New York Court of Appeals and other federal, state, and international material.

Another impressive academic site is based at the **University of Texas** and calls itself the Internet Legal Resource Guide. Two pages of particular interest included here are a list of Law Related Newsgroups and a list of Other Peoples' Lists of Law Firms and Lawyers on the Internet. Both of these are USA-based, of course.

Other organisations

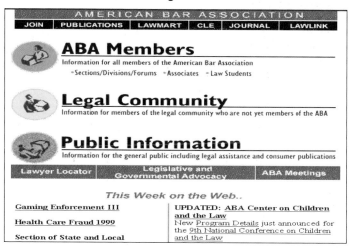

The **American Bar Association** site includes information about the ABA itself, including its own divisions, forums, groups and events. There are references to other government, academic and commercial resources and a series of items of current legal interest.

There is also a good Technology Column, written by US legal IT guru Josh Blackman, which covers many of the topics also of interest to UK and Irish lawyers.

There is a list of Law-related Internet books, and a Law Mart where legal products are sold.

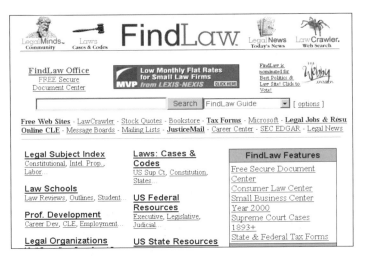

FindLaw is a widely respected and quoted legal research tool which can be used in several ways:

- as a set of resources as you can see from the picture;

- as a search engine which essentially uses other main engines to do the real work but then 'filters' the results according to whether there is legal material included; within the search process, the filter can be extended to only provide UK, or any other country's sources;

- as a set of articles and items of news, in magazine style.

The **Internet Lawyer**, is a monthly newsletter focussing on the practical use of the Internet by the legal industry. In addition to the printed newsletter (which has to be paid for) these pages provide a set of articles on legal topics, a Dr Internet advice column and a set of links to other legal resources.

A site called **Law Guru** – really the law offices of attorneys Eslamboly & Barlavi – offers information on sexual harassment, disability discrimination, workers' compensation cases (accidents at work), automobile accidents, and small claims. There is also a legal search engine set up with access to 200+ legal search engines and facilities to assist the user to subscribe over 150+ legal mailing lists. Questions can also be submitted to the attorneys for a direct answer.

Other citizen-oriented websites are provided by **Nolo Press** and **Martindale-Hubbell**.

Canada

Links to Canadian sites are at www.venables.co.uk/legal/canada.htm

Canadians generally hate Canada to be thought of as a mere adjunct to the USA and their internet presence is distinctly different from that of their southerly neighbour. Their sources are much less pretty than US sites, but the basic legal materials are nevertheless well advanced. Note, incidentally, that all official legal material is provided in both French and English.

The **Department of Justice of Canada** provides a good starting point for Canadian resources and, in particular, provides Consolidated Statutes and Regulations brought up to the consolidated state every few months.

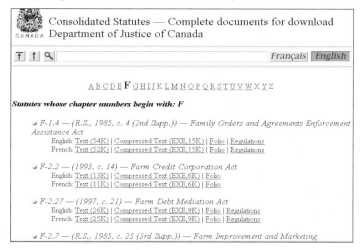

The **Parliamentary Site** covers ongoing Bills in the House of Commons or the Senate and information generally about Parliament and MPs.

The **Supreme Court of Canada** provides free Internet access to all Supreme Court of Canada decisions since January 1989. This service is provided through a joint project between the Supreme Court of Canada and the LexUM team of the Centre de Recherche en Droit Public at University of Montreal.

Despite the fact that there are a number of key official legal sites available, the best way to find your way through the Canadian system is almost certainly to use the wonderful set of links provided by **Judith Bowers** QC.

Another personal, but very useful, set of resources is provided by research lawyer **Catherine Best**. This site (naturally called the Best Guide to Canadian Legal Research) uses the skills of a teacher to assist researchers to find what they want.

The **Access to Justice Network** (ACJNet) partially funded by the Department of Justice of Canada, provides the public with legal information and educational resources from across the country.

Centre de recherche en droit public offers a collection of documents useful to the legal community and all those interested by Canadian law. At the moment the site is only in French, but an English version is on the way.

A large Canadian legal database called **QuickLaw** covers links to cases and legal documents in Canada and elsewhere. There are over 1,100 searchable databases and bulletin boards of full text judgments from all court levels and many administrative tribunals in Canada, as well as full text databases of legislation, tax and news. This is a subscription service. A disadvantage is that the service is still basically a teletype (non-Windows) service, despite the fact that you can access it over the internet. This will probably change before too long.

Class Online is a Criminal Law Search System with access to Canadian Criminal Judgements (full text), Periodicals and Factums (full text).

Australia and New Zealand

Links to Australian and New Zealand sites are at www.venables.co.uk/legal/australi.htm

Australia

Australian Capital Territory

- Administrative Appeals Tribunal of the Australian Capital Territory Decisions 1996- NEW
- Supreme Court of the Australian Capital Territory Decisions 1986-
- Australian Capital Territory Consolidated Acts and Ordinances UPDATE
- Australian Capital Territory Consolidated Regulations UPDATED
- Australian Capital Territory Numbered Acts and Ordinances UPDATED
- Australian Capital Territory Numbered Regulations UPDATED

Commonwealth

- High Court of Australia Decisions 1947-
- High Court of Australia Transcripts 1996-
- High Court of Australia Bulletins 1995-
- Administrative Appeals Tribunal Decisions 1976-
- Australian Industrial Relations Commission Decisions 1988-1996
- Australian Competition Tribunal Decisions 1997- NEW
- Australian Designs Offices Decisions 1983-
- Australian Patent Offices Decisions 1981-
- Australian Trade Marks Offices Decisions 1991-
- Copyright Tribunal Decisions 1997- NEW
- Family Court of Australia Decisions 1988-
- Federal Court of Australia Decisions 1977-
- Human Rights and Equal Opportunity Commission Decisions 1985-
- Immigration Review Tribunal Decisions 1990- UPDATED

The **Australian Legal Information Institute** (AustLII) provides free access to Australian legal materials and is definitely the place to start for any search on Australian law. In fact, it is one of the largest sources of legal materials anywhere on the net, with over six gigabytes of raw text materials and over a million searchable documents. The collection contains full-text databases of most Australian decisions and legislation. Current databases include Commonwealth, ACT, Northern Territory, Victorian, Western Australian, NSW and SA legislation and regulations, most federal courts (High Court, Federal Court, Family Court, AAT etc) and most state courts and tribunals. There are also specialised, subject specific databases.

AustLII is operated jointly by the Faculties of Law at the University of Technology, Sydney (UTS) and the University of New South Wales (UNSW). It is funded by grants of around $0.5 million per year from the Australian Research Council, the Law Foundation of New South Wales, the Council for Aboriginal Reconciliation, the Department of Foreign Affairs and Trade and other bodies.

Foundation Law is an initiative of the Law Foundation of New South Wales and provides a wide range of legal material both nationally and internationally. The full text of Federal and State law is presented as well as bills, digests, law reports and weekly Hansard. Various Australian legal directories (led by those of New South Wales) are also available. As a topical feature, there is a special page on the Olympics of Year 2000 and Olympic sports law generally.

The **Australian Commonwealth Government** presents a large amount of information on its departments, agencies and official publications. There are also links to State resources and other major Australian sites.

Lawnet, an Australian publisher, offers a data base of Federal and High Court cases and a variety of other legal services and links.

The **New South Wales Law Society** is probably the most advanced of the State Law Societies and offers a Directory of Legal Practices, a database of Members of the Law Society, the *Law Society Journal* online and an archive since 1995, information on its services and activities and a wide ranging set of links to Australian and international legal resources.

One generally has the impression, looking at Australian legal resources on the web, that the country has seized the opportunity of making itself available and noteworthy in the new technology and indeed in taking a lead in internet terms.

Major firm **Gilbert & Tobin** provides a large number of articles online relating to IT and media topics, with particular relevance to Australia (but not limited to Australian significance). These seem to be kept well up to date.

New Zealand

The **University of Waikato** Law Library, lists the Courts, Tribunals, Statutory Authorities, and such other bodies in New Zealand which make legal or quasi-legal decisions and reports. It also provides, or links to, brief information on their jurisdiction; governing legislation; administering bodies; contact details; the availability of reported (published) and unreported (unpublished) decisions; information on indexes to the decisions; and library holdings of decisions.

Directory of Decisions

Courts ▼	This site aims to list the Courts, Tribunals, Statutory Authorities, and other such
Tribunals ▼	bodies in New Zealand which make legal or quasi-legal decisions and reports.
Authorities ▼	
Commissioners & Conciliators ▼	It provides, or links to, brief information on their jurisdiction; governing legislation; administering bodies; contact details; the availability of reported
Ombudsmen ▼	(published) and unreported (unpublished) decisions; information on indexes to the
Boards ▼	decisions; and library holdings of decisions.
Case Indexes ▼	The site contains frames and Java script. It works best in Netscape Navigator 3.0 or
Law Reports ▼	higher.
Services ▼	Information on the bodies listed is obtained by contacting them directly; from
Libraries ▼	relevant legislation; from New Zealand Government Online; and the *Directory of Official Information 1997 - 1999* published by the Ministry of Justice, 1997

Links to full text legislation are made to the GP Print Collection of New Zealand Statutes on the Knowledge Basket.

The **New Zealand Government** site is a cheerful and well designed site providing information for ordinary people (eg the Citizen's Guide to Government) as well as professionals. All current consultation papers are on the site and comments invited. There is a useful set of NZ legal links here.

Legal publishers **Brookers** offer Court of Appeal Judgments from November 1995 onwards (free). New decisions will usually be included within two weeks of the date of judgment. There is also a section of current legal news and a lawyers' directory.

The **Knowledge Basket** is another source of New Zealand legal materials, some of which are available free and some on subscription. The NZ Hansard is available here and free access to NZ Acts since March 1997.

The **New Zealand Law Society** provides information about the New Zealand legal system as well as information directly for its members.

The **Auckland District Law Society** provides a basis of contact and information to the legal community there. There is a also good set of links to Commonwealth law bodies and also a current legal news section.

Finding More International Resources

Links to sites in this section are at www.venables.co.uk/legal/internat.htm

With the rapid expansion of legal resources on the internet worldwide, it is extremely difficult to identify all the key legal resources available, even in one particular country. It is certainly beyond the abilities of any one individual or organisation to keep track of every new site in the world as it emerges, and then assess it, categorise it, and link to it in an informative manner.

The best compendium sites seem to be those which are the project of a particular individual in a particular country, and these sites remain useful just as long, and only as long, as that individual is able to devote the enormous resources necessary to keeping the project up to date.

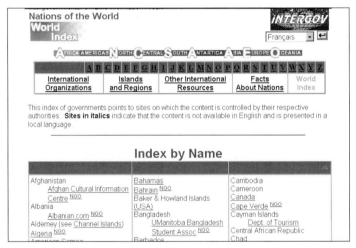

An Index of Government Sites, worldwide, provided by the Canada-based **Intergov** organisation, gives links to the Governmental site, and basic (brief) information about absolutely every country in the world. You can also take a cross-section of the information according to whether you are interested in Africa, North America, Central America, South America, Antarctica, Asia, Europe and Oceana. There are also lists of international organisations both by topic and by name.

The **CIA World Fact Book** gives detailed information about all these countries, including maps. An astounding resource.

International Law

- **The International Court of Justice**
- **International Criminal Court -
  Post-conference developments**
  · Diplomatic Conference (June-July 1998, Rome, Italy)
- **Codification, Development and
  Promotion of International Law**
- **International Law Commission**
- **International Trade Law**

- **Law of the Sea**
- **Treaties**
- **International Criminal Tribunal for the
  Former Yugoslavia (ICTY)**
- **International Criminal Tribunal for Rwanda
  (ICTR)** (Arusha)
  **Verdicts on the crime of genocide by the
  International Criminal Tribunal for Rwanda
  (ICTR)**

- **United Nations Documentation Research
  Guide: special section on international law**

The **United Nations** provides an International Law collection of sources, treaties, courts, tribunals and links. The **United Nations Commission on International Trade Law** (UNCITRAL), the core legal body of the United Nations in the field of International Trade Law, also provides a set of links.

There is a comprehensive index to International law sources on the **Australian Legal Information Institute** (AustLII) site.

The **Auckland District Law Society** provides a also good set of links to Commonwealth law bodies and law sources in particular.

Another extensive set of international references has been set up at **Osaka University** called the World Law Resource List.

An extensive Foreign Law Collection is maintained by the **University of Southern California**. There are subsections for each country.

Indiana University School of Law at Bloomington, USA, provides a set of pointers to legal resources around the world, including search tools and lists of material by subject and by source.

The **International Court of Justice** (ICJ) at the Hague provides full text judgments since 1996 and other material.

Lex Mercatoria is a collection of resources for international commercial law and e-commerce provided by the **University of Tromsø**, Norway and three other collaborating universities. It provides access to a large collection of treaties, conventions, model laws and documents.

Index